I AM
THE
ETERNAL LIFE

GRACE DOLA BALOGUN

I AM THE ETERNAL LIFE
Copyright ©2013 Grace Dola Balogun

Contact Author at:
www.Gracereligiousbookspublishers.com
1-646-559-2533

Grace Religious Books Publishing & Distributors books may be ordered through booksellers or by contacting the publisher:

Grace Religious Books Publishing & Distributors, Inc.
New York
213 Bennett Avenue
New York, NY 10040

All rights reserved. No part of this book may be used or reproduced by any means, graphic, electronic, or mechanical, including photocopying, recording, taping or by any information storage retrieval system without the written permission of the publisher except in the case of brief quotations embodied in critical articles and reviews.

Because of the dynamic nature of the Internet, any web addresses or links contained in this book may have changed since publication and may no longer be valid. The views expressed in this work are solely those of the author and do not necessarily reflect the views of the publisher, and the publisher hereby disclaims any responsibility for them.

The author of this book does not dispense medical advice or prescribe the use of any technique as for treatment for physical, emotional, or medical problems without the advice of a physician, either directly or indirectly. The intent of the author is only to offer information of a general nature to help you in your quest for emotional and spiritual well-being. In the event you use any of the information in this book for yourself, which is your constitutional right, the author and the publisher assume no responsibility for your actions.

Soft Cover: 9781939415196
Hard Cover: 9781939415233

Library of Congress Control Number: 2013932122

Editing and Interior Design by CBM Christian Book Marketing www.christian-book-marketing.com
Cover Design by Lisa Hainline @ www.lisahainline.com

Printed in the United States of America
Grace Religious Books Publishing & Distributors, Inc.
New York

I AM THE ETERNAL LIFE

DEDICATION

I dedicate this book to God, the Father Almighty, God the Son, and God the Holy Spirit who are forever one God. Who through the eternal Spirit teaches us that we must worship God in Spirit and in truth. Jesus Christ, His begotten Son teaches that one must come to God in complete sincerity and with a spirit that is directed by the life and activity of the Holy Spirit. Christ as the attribute of God the Father, just as our words and thoughts come from us and cannot be separated from us, in the same way Jesus Christ cannot be separated from the Father. Christ as the Word of God, the speech of God, Christ the living Word of God who lives forevermore. In Christ there is eternal life through the redemptive work of God the Father and the power of God.

I also dedicate this book to those who will read it and acquire great wisdom and knowledge to believe that in

Christ, the righteousness of God has been revealed from faith to faith. They will live by faith to the point that they will give their lives to the One and only the Word of God and God, who only is the eternal life and everlasting life from this Earth to Heaven.

To all the people on Earth that seek after their own life, and finally one day they will come to the knowledge and understanding of the eternal life before they leave this Earth, may they know that eternal life is only in Jesus Christ. Believe in Him and you will live forever with Him in Heaven.

CONTENTS

DEDICATION 5
PREFACE 9

CHAPTER ONE 13
Eternal Life Beginning From The Old Testament

CHAPTER TWO 23
Jesus Christ Extends Eternal Life To The Samaritan Woman

CHAPTER THREE 31
Jesus Christ Teaches Eternal Life To Nicodemus

CHAPTER FOUR 41
The Power of Eternal Life

CHAPTER FIVE 51
Eternal Life From Earth To Heaven

CHAPTER SIX 61
Eternal Life That They May Know You As The One And Only True God

CHAPTER SEVEN 67
Eternal Life: The Joy of the Believers

CHAPTER EIGHT 71
Jesus Christ: The Source of Eternal Life

CHAPTER NINE 77
Eternal Life Encouragement To Believers

CHAPTER TEN 81
Eternal Glory

CHAPTER ELEVEN 87
Assurance of Eternal Life

CHAPTER TWELVE 91
From Earth to Life Eternal

CHAPTER THIRTEEN 97
Gift of Eternal Life

CHAPTER FOURTEEN 105
Forever Live With God

CHAPTER FIFTEEN 113
Awareness of God In Our Lives

SUMMARY 117

PRAYER 123
--of an Intercessor for Believers

BIBLIOGRAPHY 125

BIBLICAL INDEX 127

ABOUT THE AUTHOR 140

ORDER FORM 142

PREFACE

Eternal life is a very important theme in the New Testament, although not without the Old Testament history of eternal or everlasting life. Eternal life is therefore, one of the unifying themes of the New Testament. Eternal life explains and describes the salvation that God the Father bestowed upon those who have faith and those who trust, as well as, serve the Lord Jesus Christ. Eternal life reveals the time that God's unmerited favor extends to His people and the Word is reality of His existence, so that they may enjoy and rejoice, as they worship and serve Him.

People of this world have misunderstood the meaning of eternal life in the Scriptures because they base it in, "Born again saved and always saved." These words have nothing to do with eternal life. Eternal life is based primarily on life that is from God, since God is always the eternal. Eternal life will always be eternal life whether the people of this Earth believe in God or not or whatever religion they may believe in. Trust in God and give your life to God; eternal life will always be eternal since God is the main source of eternal life. People can possess it only through faith and intimate relationship with God and His Son, Jesus Christ.

The Book of Psalms says, "Before the mountains were formed or you brought forth the earth and the world, from everlasting to everlasting you are God" (Psalm 90:2). Moses prayed this prayer to God; knowledge and power filled him, more than he could imagine and he saw clearly that God is eternal. Moses refers to God's eternal existence, having neither beginning nor an end. Everlasting does not mean that God transcends time, but rather emphasized His endless duration in time. God knows the past as past, the present as present, and the future as future. Moses said, before the beginning of time thou had being; we may take comfort from God's immortality. Since God is always eternal; eternal life is from Him; it is a life that God ordained, possesses and issues because God alone and only possesses immortality.

Moses was in the wilderness and prayed this prayer in the mist of all of what he was going through he knew that God was the only answer. He finds relief in the eternity of God; he knew that God is unchanging and that

He is a home and a refuge for his people from eternity and to all eternity. God has infinite love, wisdom, power, holiness, is full of justice, goodness, grace and truth. God is unchangeable, He is the same yesterday, today and forever, He is God. "I will be glad and rejoice in you; I will sing praise to your name, O Most High" (Psalm 9:2).

"For God so loved the world that he gave his one and only Son, that whoever believes in him shall not perish but have eternal Life" (John 3:16). God showed His love to humanity through sending His only Son to the world; this act reveals the heart and purpose of God. God's love is unchanging and wide enough to embrace all the people in the world. God gave His Son as atonement for our sin on the Cross. The Atonement precedes from the loving heart of the Almighty God the Father.

Eternal life is the divine gift that is bestowed upon those who believe in Jesus Christ through God. It is the blessedness in God's presence that endures forever. It relates to the quality of life of believers in Jesus Christ on this Earth or from this Earth to Heaven. It is also relates to both the quality of the believers' life and duration of the future life. We have to understand the meaning of eternal life from the Old Testament.

The people of this world will receive eternal life through Jesus who is Lord and Savior of this world. The reason is that believing in Jesus Christ as the only Son of God and the Savior, the one who died, was buried and raised to life again for my sins, and the sins of the entire people on this Earth. No one can have eternal life without making Jesus Christ their Lord and Savior, and no one can have eternal life without being born again as a new creature; old things pass away and behold all things become new to those who believe in Jesus Christ and made him their Lord and Savior by putting their trust in Him.

CHAPTER ONE

ETERNAL LIFE BEGINNING FROM OLD TESTAMENT

In the book of Deuteronomy, the Scripture says God is eternal with His Word: "The eternal God is your refuge, and underneath are the everlasting arms. He will drive out your enemy before you saying, destroy him!" (Deuteronomy 33:27). The Psalmist is saying that God is the eternal God and his arms are everlasting, He was before the universe and He will continue to be when the time and days shall be no more.

We have to see also in the Old Testament Scripture, King David says, "The Lord is King for ever and ever, the nations will perish from his land" (Psalm 10:16). The Lord is saying that the day of vengeance will arrive one day on this Earth, when the kingdoms of this world will become the kingdom of our Lord Jesus Christ. Then the wicked and persecuting nations will perish themselves according to

King David. This should be an encouragement to the believers, as well as their hope that God's will, in the manner, break the arms of those who are persecuting the Christians around the world. He will let them know that He has heard their prayers and answered their prayers. The Lord is eternal over all the enemies of the Cross.

Another scripture in the Old Testament says, "For this God is our God for ever and ever, he will be our guide even to the end" (Psalm 48:14). The Scripture is saying to us that the Lord has committed Himself to be the believer's faithful and constant guide throughout life, in the experience of death and beyond death to the eternal home where we will be with Him forever. In this present age, injustice and evil run wild, and God sometimes appears to put his face aside and not interfere. God's people must pray that He will stop evil and suffering. We must be confident and well assured that though the day of justice has not arrived, the Lord has heard our prayers and will give encouragement until the end.

The Lord God Almighty has committed Himself to be the believer's faithful and constant guide throughout life, and also in the external home where we will be with Him forever. God will be our guide above death, beyond death; He will guide us safely to happiness on the other side of death, to a life in which there will be no more death, which is eternal life.

"You will keep in perfect peace him whose mind is steadfast, because he trusts in your rock eternal. Trust in the Lord forever, for the Lord, the Lord, is the Rock eternal" (Isaiah 26:3-4). In the Last Days God will keep in perfect peace the remnant that remain steadfast and faithful to their Lord Jesus Christ. In times of troubles, tribulations and persecutions, believers must trust continually in the everlasting arms of God. Believers must strive to keep their minds and hearts turned to the Lord in their prayers, keeping their trust and hope in Him. Christians must place their trust, their lives in Him because He is a rock who endures forever; He is a sure and firm foundation of all those who believe in Him.

One gospel song writer says, "Rock of ages, cleft for me, let me hide myself in thee, let the water and the blood, from thy riven side which flowed, be of sin the double cure, cleanse me from its guilt and power" (Augustus M. Toplady 1776). All who believe in God are safe, have a security and serenity of mind in the assurance of God's favor. God keeps and bless His people with an inward peace, outward peace, peace with God, peace of conscience, and peace in all circumstances. Christians must trust our Lord and Savior. Their minds and hearts must be stayed upon Him 24/7; by doing so, God will then keep them in perpetual peace. That peace will help them to put their trust in Him forever, when earthly troubles are present in their lives.

Whenever people put their trust on earthly things it has a time limit, but when we put our trust in the Lord, it will last as long as we shall last, or as long as we live on this Earth. The Lord Jesus Christ, God the Father, Son and Holy Spirit who was, and is, and is to come, is the Rock eternal, a firm and lasting foundation of the faith building of every Christian and the house that was built on the rock will stand on any storms of the world. Eternal life is rooted in God's Word, Will, His being and is likewise eternal.

Believers must be confident that God will accomplish His redemptive purpose; the saints break out into praise and prayer. Their song concerns God's triumphant destruction of all evil and the establishment of His kingdom on Earth. When the trying and stressful days of the end of history occur, God will keep in perfect peace the remnant that remain steadfast and faithful to their Lord. In times of trouble we must continually strive to keep our minds turned to the Lord in prayer, putting our trust and hope in Him. We must place our trust on Jesus because He is a rock who endures forever; he is our sure and firm foundation.

"But the Lord is the true God; he is the living God, the eternal King. When he is angry, the earth trembles, the Nations cannot endure his wrath" (Jeremiah 10:10). Prophet Jeremiah warns the people of Israel against worshiping idols and all ungodly manners, or actions that can easily move them far away from God. He declared to them that the Lord God is the one true God who created all things. Prophet Jeremiah's warnings apply to the people of this world today as well. He lets us know that believers should not let earthly problems or troubles turn them to idols, astrology and spiritism, which surrounded the people in all the nations of this world.

Many people in the world do the same thing today. Instead of seeking God with their trials and tribulations, they trust in idols. They must know that the Lord and Savior is the Savior over all the troubles on Earth. Our Lord is the One true God who created all things, the sea and everything that dwells in it, He makes all things complete. The manufacturer of all the idols will perish together with their images of the idols. They are the works of men's hands, and our Lord and Savior is the God of truth. He is the God of truth and He is the living Savior.

He is the God of Abraham, Isaac and Jacob who lives forever more. He is life, has life in Himself and is the fountain of life to all His creations. Idols can be broken and destroyed, but our Lord and Savior lives forever who has immortality in the light. He is the God of nature, the fountain of all beings and all powers of nature such as – thunder, storms and earthquakes are at His command. The entire universe has its origin in Him. God made us and He made all things. He created the Earth and its valuable treasure with His infinite power.

"I will hasten and not delay to obey your commands" (Psalm 119:60). God wants all those who believe in Him to obey His command, and hasten to obey His Word and do them. "Your word, O Lord, is eternal; it stands firm in the heavens" (Psalm 119:89). God's Word is rooted in His Word, His Will and in His being; is likewise eternal the same as His righteous Laws and His ways. The Bible is the inspired word of God and is the message communicated by God to the people of this world. God's wisdom and character will never change. The Word of God is life and lives forever; the Word of God is God.

David acknowledges the unchangeableness of the Word of God and he says Lord, "Your Word is the same there is no variableness in you and you proof it by your

Word. With your Word heavens were made, you established the earth; you fulfilled your promise to Noah" (Genesis 6:1-22). All your creatures are in their places, and accordingly, believers receive wisdom and power of the Spirit indwelling through Jesus Christ when they put their faith in Him and surrender all to His Lordship.

The Old Testament Scripture witnesses and bears testimony to the Word of God which was incarnate in Jesus Christ. There is not likely to be much difficulty in identifying the incarnate Word with the word that the apostles proclaim. Eternal life is a timeless existence; it is eternal and has no end.

All believers of Jesus Christ, immediately after their conversion, God's Word must be received, believed and obeyed as the final authority in all things pertaining to life and godliness. God's Word must be used in the church as the final authority in all matters for teaching, rebuking correcting and training in righteous living. One cannot submit to Jesus Christ's lordship without submitting to God and His Word as the ultimate authority. The Scripture can only be understood when we are in a right relationship to the Holy Spirit. The Holy Spirit will open our minds to understand the meaning of the Scripture, as well as, give us the inward witness of its authority.

We have to look at the prayer of the Prophet Habakkuk, "He stood, and shook the earth; he looked, and made the nations tremble. The ancient mountains crumbled and the age-old hills collapsed. His ways are eternal" (Habakkuk 3:6). Prophet Habakkuk reminded the people of Israel when God delivered them from the land of slavery in Egypt. The Scripture is telling us that the same God who came with salvation in the past would come again in all His glory. All who were waiting for that coming would live and see His triumph over empires and nations.

The Old Testament does not conceive of eternity in pure terms as a state of timelessness. In the world history, the view of eternity is a motionless, changeless state, remote, qualitatively distinct from time. Time and eternity are antithetical and eternity is accessible to humans, though only by logical speculation that views God not as the personal living, historically, self-revealing being described in the Scripture.

The Old Testament resists time, eternity and speaks of a coming age from which evil will be banished, in which God's life and glory will be determined for all who exist in the world. This is different from the current world order. But that age has points of continuity with the present one because the God of that age is the same as the God of this present age.

God is allowing the presence of Satan and evil in this present age until they meet their final end. God's reign extends for all time and over all times. This means that the temporal order of redemptive potential as the sphere in which God's Spirit, the Spirit of the incarnate and risen Lord works out His will in human affairs. History cannot fully contain the reality of the transcendent God and also is not in capable of receiving or responding to His presence.

The incarnation of Jesus Christ offers the abundant proof of this fact. While eternity lies chronologically beyond temporal life in this Earth and present time now, we have to look at the revelation of God's presence in and intent for both the present world order and the coming world order. The Old Testament, then, encourages us to define eternity in terms of the duration of the revealed God's dealings with His people in times past, now and always. God has ever been solicitous for His name and for the people with whom He has ordained. God's past state affairs will continue for eternity, as long as God who lives and loves endures.

To deeply define eternity more clearly, believers must have a personal relationship with God and trust Him by realizing what eternal life signifies, to live our life responsively before Him and to gain understanding with wisdom into eternal life.

CHAPTER TWO

JESUS CHRIST EXTENDS ETERNAL LIFE TO THE SAMARITAN WOMAN

Jesus was traveling from Judea to Galilee through Samaria because there was no other route. We have to know that it has been written that the Son of God must reveal Himself to the people of Samaria through a simple, lowly and insignificant woman that nobody recognized in the village. Up till today our Lord and Savior always reveals Himself to people that nobody would recognize or pay no mind to, un-famous people and the poor to achieve His purpose of salvation.

Jesus Christ preached His first sermon to the woman by telling the woman all that she has done and the woman became the first missionary to go to her village to tell everyone about Jesus. Everyone in her village rushed to Jesus and they heard the Word of God; they rejoiced and were saved. Even though Jesus was weary on His journey and was physically tired, he was strong in the Spirit and he was fully, but still fully divine. Poor as He was, He was unable to travel by any other means other than by walking.

We believers must think about all what our Savior has gone through in other to bring us to eternal life. His disciples went to the village to get food. While He was waiting, He was supplied with a spiritual food, which is the food from His Father. The Father is always with His Son Christ just as Christ is always with us today. He did not go to the village to fetch food because he knew a divine providence that would bring about glorious purposes that was awaiting that seems to us as accidental, although it is never accidental. Everything works together according to the divine plan and purpose of the Almighty God.

He had been preaching to multitudes, but this particular day He condescends to teach and preach to a single woman; This woman is a poor woman, a disliked woman in the village and a friendless woman because she came to the well alone to draw water. This means that she did not have friends in the village that might be due to her life style of association with five different men. This woman happened to be a Samaritan woman that the Jews did not associate with.

I AM THE ETERNAL LIFE

We believers must do the same today. We must reach out to the poor and lowly in our ministry of the Gospel of God. We must minister to the unreachable and the people in the most dangerous and rural areas. When or if we do this, it will bring us a glorious achievement of saving one sinner unto the hands of our Lord. The Scripture says, "In the same way, I tell you, there is rejoicing in the presence of the angels of God over one sinner who repents" (Luke 15:10). This verse is telling us that God and the angels in Heaven have such love, compassion and grief for those who have fallen into sin and spiritual death, that when one sinner repents, they openly rejoice.

When a Samaritan woman came to draw water, Jesus said to her, "Will you give me a drink"? (His disciples had gone into the town to buy food). The Samaritan woman said to Him, 'You are a Jew and I am Samaritan woman. How can you ask me for a drink?' (For Jews do not associate with Samaritans). Jesus answered her, "If you know the gift of God and who it is that asks you for a drink, you would have asked him and he would have given you a living water. "Sir", the woman said, "you have nothing to draw with and the well is deep. Where can you get this living water? Are you greater than our Father

Jacob, who gave us the well and drank from it himself, as did also his sons and his flocks and herds?" Jesus answered, "Everyone who drinks this water will be thirsty again, but whoever drinks the water I give him will never thirst, indeed, the water I give him will become in him a Spring of water welling up to eternal life" (John 4: 7-14). Jesus Christ extended eternal life to the Samaritan woman during the conversation with her. The God of glory reveals Himself in so many ways to the people of this world. During our Lord's earthly ministry, he did a lot of miracles, for example He healed diseases, fed the poor and brought life again to the dead. Jesus' conversation to the Samaritan woman reveals His commitment to His heavenly Father's purpose and His own inner desire to bring people to eternal life.

    Jesus Christ's consuming passion was to save the sinner and the lost. This is more important to Him than the food that His disciples went out to buy. We believers of Jesus Christ must follow in His footsteps by making the things of God our number one priority. By winning souls into His Holy hands, this is one of the ways we seek the Kingdom above all that is in our lives. All around the world people are thirsty for the truth of God and His word. People that sit in the shadow of darkness need the light of

Jesus to shine in their lives. Jesus Christ is the light of this world; we must make Him known wherever we are and in whatever we do.

We must find ways to speak to the people about their spiritual need about Jesus. He is the only one that can fulfill people of this world's spiritual needs. Jesus Christ said to the Samaritan woman and presented eternal life to her in a simple way by "water" which means spiritual life - the living water that everyone that comes to the world must drink. This activity of drinking is not momentary or a one-time activity, but rather a progressive or repeated drinking. Drinking the water of life requires regular communion with the source of the living water, Jesus Christ Himself. No one can continue to drink the water of life if he or she becomes severed from its source. Such people will become, as Peter describes it, "springs without water" (2nd Peter 2:17).

Our Lord opens the conversation by approaching the woman with a request for water. Christ is still requesting us sinners and unbelievers to open their hearts and let Him in. We love Him because He loved us first. Christ said whoever gives a cup of water to the needy in His name will always be rewarded. The Samaritan woman was surprised and amazed that Jesus who is a Jew was asking her for water. The woman was surprised because she knew that Jewish people were full of pride. They would rather endure hardship or die than asking or begging a Samaritan for anything in those ancient times. Jesus Christ is telling us today to be like Him in order to save souls. We must put our pride down, our position, our wealth and humble ourselves in order to reach the lost and the sinners.

We must put on all the fruits of the Spirit, which are goodness, kindness, love and peace. Jesus Christ used this occasion to introduce the Gospel to her through His revealing of divine truth. Jesus Christ's goal was to let this woman knows that He is the awaiting Messiah. He fills her heart with an apprehension that now she has the opportunity of gaining that which would be of an unspeakable advantage to her spiritually.

He let her know that in Him nothing is impossible, especially a living water which is the Holy Spirit who is like water in the bottom of the well, as well as like living or running water. The Spirit and of grace of God is living water. Jesus Christ is the only one who can and will give the Holy Spirit to those who believed in Him and ask Him for it. The fountain of life is hid from people of this world; it can only be found in Christ. Jesus Christ has enough living water for His people. The Spirit is the running water that leads to eternal life in Him.

The woman was telling Jesus that this very well was where the Patriarch Jacob drank from himself and so did his children and all his cattle as well. This shows that the power of God's providence with the continuation of the fountains of water, food and all other needs from generation to generation. God never fails; He is always there to provide and meet all of our needs if he knows that it is good for us. Jesus Christ did not condemn the woman, but encouraged her by letting her know that the water of Jacob's well can only quench physical thirst, but her spiritual thirst is the same as any ordinary water in the world. It can only quench the present thirst, after that she will come back again and again.

Jesus Christ assured the Samaritan woman that the living water that He gives will yield a lasting satisfaction, and those who drink of it will never thirst again. Jesus Christ is the truth and to live in union with Christ requires speaking the truth with love. Today believers of Jesus Christ have in them a well of water that is overflowing and ever flowing; it is always springing up and always in motion. The truth of God in our spirit, soul and body is like standing water spring up into everlasting life, which helps believers to aim, think good, do good and follow the Lord. It is a spiritual life that helps believers towards perfection in eternal life. It will continue to be springing up until it comes to perfection of eternal life forever.

CHAPTER THREE

JESUS CHRIST TEACHES ETERNAL LIFE TO NICODEMUS

Jesus Christ teaches Nicodemus about Eternal Life. Nicodemus, a Jewish a member of the ruling council, came to Jesus at night. Nicodemus was called by God because he listened to Jesus Christ's teaching and he followed all His teachings from time to time. He must have disguised himself or sent someone to write all what Christ was teaching down. One day he was full of confusion about one of the important teachings of Jesus. He does not want to visit Him in the day in order to avoid criticisms from the Pharisees Jewish council.

Nicodemus decided to visit Jesus at night because of so many questions that he wanted to ask of Him. Let us read the Scripture, "Now there was a man of the Pharisees named Nicodemus, a member of the Jewish ruling Council. He came to Jesus at night and said, 'Rabbi, we know you are a teacher who has come from God. For no one could perform the miraculous signs you are doing if God were not with him. In reply Jesus declared, 'I tell you the truth, no one can see the Kingdom of God unless he is born again.' 'How can a man be born when he is old? How can a man be born when he is old?' Nicodemus asked. 'Surely he cannot enter a second time into his mother's womb to be born.' "

Jesus answered, " 'I tell you the truth, no one can enter the kingdom of God unless he is born of water and the Spirit. Flesh gives birth to flesh, but the spirit gives birth to spirit. You should not be surprised at my saying, you must be born again. The wind blows wherever it pleases. You hear its sound, but you cannot tell where it comes from or where it is going. So it is with every one born of the Spirit' 'How can this be?' Nicodemus asked.".(John 3:1-9). Nicodemus did not want to interrupt Jesus or he might have made his visit at night just to avoid the Pharisees condemnation. He did not want the chief priest to know about his visit to Christ because he does not want them to be angrier at Jesus. He preferred to see Christ at night and gain knowledge while other people were sleeping.

Some rich people do this as well. For instance some presidents of a nation will call pastors and ministers to pray for them and they will go to them for answers to their questions about the power of God over certain situations. Nicodemus did not have the knowledge about how many days Christ would be staying in Jerusalem so therefore, he quickly made a night visit. Nicodemus believes that at night he will be able to have a one to one conversation with Jesus Christ. It is the same with some believers today. We communicate with the Lord at night than in the daytime, because of the many distractions that goes on in the day.

Conversing with Christ would be freer, less liable to disturbances. Jesus welcomes him whole heartedly. There is no time we approach the King of kings, He always has time for those who seek Him with boldness and from the bottom of their hearts. Jesus Christ will accept us, pardon all our transgressions and taught us to encourage people that are weak, ashamed and afraid. After believers were converted they always boldly proclaimed the name of Christ publicly. It was the same with Nicodemus during the burial of our Lord and Savior Jesus Christ. Nicodemus was no longer afraid and no longer feared, nor cared what the chief priest would say because he had been born again.

Nicodemus called Jesus Christ "Rabbi" which means a great spiritual man. Even today those who have hope and respect for Jesus and think highly honorably of Christ, will receive a reward from this Earth to Heaven. Nicodemus supports his question to Jesus with a supported divine inspirational authority. He knows that Christ is a great teacher, one that can rule by the power of grace and truth. Here we have Nicodemus with a judicious sensibility, and inquisitively, he is someone that has had the opportunity to examine what Christ had been teaching. He was fully satisfied with all of Christ's miracles and healings that Christ brought forth upon the people. Believers of Jesus Christ must do the same today by reviewing and reading the Bible to see what Christ has done and acknowledge His power of the Word of God.

If we study Christ's ministry at all times, we are to receive Him as a teacher that comes from God and introduced Him to other people around us that do not know Him. It was not enough for Nicodemus to admire only Christ's works of healing and miracles, but we must acknowledge His mission to save sinners and the lost, all must be born again. Jesus Christ told Nicodemus that he can have no benefit unless there is a change in his spirit through the Spirit of God. Jesus Christ explained the doctrine of the Christian faith, which is Spiritual birth, without the new birth, one cannot see the Kingdom of God, and receive eternal life and salvation.

The important facts of a new birth are in regeneration. Regeneration is a re-creating of spiritual life according to the Scriptures in the human heart by God and the Holy Spirit. The new birth cannot be compared with the physical birth. God the Father's relationship with believers of Jesus Christ is a matter of Spirit not of flesh. Therefore, while the physical tie of a father and child cannot be annulled, the Father and child relationship that God desires and requires from us is a relationship voluntarily offered by believers and not indissoluble during our probationary period on Earth.

The relationship that remains conditional and one that is based on our faith in Christ our Lord and Savior through our earthly existence, after which is demonstrated by lives of sincere love and obedience. "Therefore, brothers we have an obligation but it is not to the sinful nature, to live according to the sinful nature, you will die, but if by the spirit you put to death the misdeeds of the body, you will live, because those who are led by the Spirit of God are Sons of God" (Romans 8:12-14). Because of sin and its ravaging effects, the body in the natural state is under the process and sentence of death, even for the believer.

Our bodies ultimately will be redeemed by the resurrection or transformation at Jesus Christ's Second Coming. Jesus came to give us life here and now, the Holy Spirit who raised Jesus Christ from the dead will impart life to our "mortal bodies" and believers must welcome the Holy Spirit into their hearts; the Holy Spirit is the Spirit of life.

Apostle Paul explained and emphasized the necessity for continual warfare against all the people of God, that this warfare would limit God's work in our lives if we do not focus on Jesus. If believers refuses to put to death the misdeeds of the body, believers might pass through spiritual life back into spiritual death. Therefore, the life of God that believers received at new birth can be extinguished in the soul of a believer who refuses to put to death the misdeeds of the body (Romans 8:13).

We must be born again; we must live a new life in Jesus Christ. Birth is the beginning of life, to be born again is the beginning of a spiritual life. We have a new nature, new principles to this way of life and new affections. What affected us before we were born again will no longer affect us, what was very important to us, before we were born again will no longer important to us anymore. We will have a new aim and a new goal to live on this Earth. We will be born a new creature on Earth and from Heaven above. Our souls will be glued to Jesus Christ. It is a new birth, which will rise up to Heaven and descend from Heaven is divine. This heavenly life will fill us up on Earth.

It is a new life that the people that knew us before will see in us and praise the Father of heavenly lights. We cannot see it or understand the nature of it; we cannot receive the comfort of it unless we are born again. Regeneration is absolutely necessary to our happiness here on Earth and in Heaven. It will be shone to us clearly that we must be born again. We cannot be holy if we are not born again. This is the great truth of the regeneration that was laid down by God the Father through Jesus Christ our Lord and Savior.

Jesus Christ was speaking the spiritual truth to Nicodemus. It was a great surprise for Nicodemus to hear about this truth that was hid from the High Priest and the entire Jewish ruling council. Nicodemus surrendered willingly to be taught by Christ; he did not get angry or turn away from Christ because of his hard saying, but gently and ingenuously acknowledged his ignorance. He says,

Lord make me understand. Can a man entered his mother's womb and be born again? Because this is the only way that he knows how a man could be born again. Even today the things of God are hid to those you would expect to know it. More importantly, the things of God were dark to some people, and it is sometimes hard for them to understand it. We must continue to seek after the knowledge of God that surpasses all understanding. Nicodemus did not understand the mystery of regeneration. Jesus Christ opened up the Scriptures and further explained to him again, as well as confirmed, what He was telling Nicodemus.

It is very important that we expound and explain until the sinner and the lost understand the word of the Gospel. We must pray for a spirit of patience to be able to witness to others whenever we get into a situation such as Nicodemus. To be born again is to be born of The Spirit, not by wisdom or supernatural power of our own, but by the power and influence of the grace of God through the Holy Spirit. Jesus Christ shows Nicodemus that it is necessary to be born again due to the nature that which is born of flesh is flesh. The soul is still a spiritual substance living in the flesh, captivated and control by the will of the flesh. What type of communion can there be between God, who is a Spirit, and a Soul in this condition where the flesh is in control?

The corrupt nature which is flesh exists from our birth, the new nature which rises from our second birth with a new nature is spirit. If it is possible for Nicodemus to enter his mother's womb again and be born many, many times, it will still be born of the flesh which is flesh. This will not help Nicodemus to have close or spiritual communion with God. Sin corrupted our flesh nature. We must put on a new man and be born again by the Spirit. Jesus Christ is the Great Physician of all human souls on Earth. He said and gave a great commission that we must be born again of the Spirit, which is the ultimate cure for our sin nature.

The change that God requires comes in two folds. First, the regenerating work of the Holy Spirit is compared to water; the born again must be born of water and of Spirit. Which is primarily intended to show that the spirit sanctifying the soul cleanses and purifies the soul as water washes away all the dirty things from our body when we shower.

Washing with water, born again by water, by washing with water, as the visible sign of spiritual grace. Second, it is compared to wind. "The wind blows wherever it pleases. You hear its sound, but you cannot tell where it comes from or where it is going. So it is with everyone born of the Spirit"(John 3:8). The word wind signifies both the wind and the Spirit. The Spirit in regeneration works in so many various ways as a free agent. The Spirit operates his activities where and when, on whom, and in a different degrees of measure as He pleases. The truth that Jesus Christ communicated and taught Nicodemus made him to have a change of mind about Jesus and he believed that Christ was the Messiah. Believe in Him and be born again by His spirit, which is the spirit of life in Him.

CHAPTER FOUR

THE POWER OF ETERNAL LIFE

Eternal life refers to the power to become the children of God because of the resurrection of Jesus Christ. Eternal life is granted and conferred to those who are exulted to the highest position through faith and trust in Jesus Christ, the Son of God. It is a spiritual progress that leads to eternal life in the heavenly realm.

Obedience to the Lord involves the following of the Holy Spirit's power and movement towards God's power. This is an example to every one of us. Jesus first made us alive in Him and made us to obedient to Him through the power of the Holy Spirit. Therefore, we walk with the Lord and He speaks to us and in turn listen to all that He speaks. He reveals His love for us with a divine enable of the work of the Holy Spirit that lifts and enables our spirit to a divine communication with Jesus Christ. Jesus Christ comes to us and causes us to rise with Him.

The Scripture says that Christ is able to save those who come to Him. "Therefore, he is able to save completely those who come to God through him, because he always lives to intercede for them. Such a high priest meets our need one who is holy, blameless, pure, set apart from sinners, exalted above the heavens" (Hebrew 7:25-26). Jesus Christ lives in Heaven at the right hand of God the Father –interceding for each and every one who puts their trust in Him and follows Him according to His Father's Will. Through our Lord Jesus Christ and the ministry of intercession, we experience God's love and presence, and find mercy and grace to help in all the various times of our needs through the power of eternal life.

Jesus Christ continually pours out His Spirit on all those who believe in Him. The Spirit of the Lord Jesus Christ, the Holy Spirit, helps us to understand the content of His intercessory ministry. Our Lord said in the Scripture, "Father, the true has come, glorify your Son, that your Son may glorify you. For you granted him authority over all people that he might give eternal life to all those you have given him. Now this is eternal life that they may know you, the only true God, and Jesus Christ, whom you have sent. I have brought you glory on earth by completing the work you gave me to do. And now, Father, glorify me in your presence with the glory I had with you before the world began"(John 17:1-5).

During Jesus Christ's final hour on Earth He prayed for His disciples and for those who would believe in Him. The prayers of Jesus continue with us today as well. Our Lord Jesus Christ's prayer indicated His deepest longing of love for those who would believe in Him, then and now. It should also serve as a spirit inspired example of how all ordained pastors, ministers and reverends should pray for their people, and how Christian parents should pray for their children. In praying for those who are under our care, or those who ask us for prayers, our greatest concerns should be that they may know Jesus as Lord, Christ and His work of redemption. Our prayer should be that God would keep them from the evil of the world, never to fall into false preaching or teaching, and for the Lord to keep them away from Satan's temptations. We must pray that people under our responsibility and our care may constantly possess the fullness of joy of Jesus Christ; we also must pray that they may be holy in deeds, thought and in their character, that they may be completely one in purpose and fellowship, as demonstrated by Jesus Christ Himself and by God the Father.

The most important prayer is that they may lead people to Christ and become soul winners for the Kingdom of God. Prayers should be offered that they may persevere in faith and finally be where Christ is in Heaven so that the love that the Father has for Jesus, His only begotten Son may be in them, and that this love will transform their love to love Jesus Christ with the same fervent love that the Father loves Jesus Christ by His spirit may be with the believers.

Eternal life, which is more than endless life, is a special quality of life that we as believers receive when we partake of the essential life of God through Jesus Christ. This eternal life allows and helps us to know God in ever growing knowledge and understanding, and communion with the Father, Son and the Holy Spirit. Eternal life power is the present possession of life that requires a living faith. Eternal life is not secured and maintained merely by an act of repentance and faith, it involves the past, present, and future union and fellowship with Jesus Christ where we know for sure that there is no eternal life without the power of the ever living head, Jesus Christ. A future hope of eternal life is associated with the coming of Christ for His faithful and is contingent on our living by faith and by the Spirit.

The power of eternal life lies on Christ's word of prayer for protection, joy, sanctification, love and unity applies only to a particular people. For example to those who belong to God, by believing in Jesus Christ, which are separated from the world, as well as obey the Word of Jesus Christ, acceptance of His teachings and putting their total trust in Him. Jesus Christ will sanctify them and make them holy and set them apart from the world. They must be separated from the world and sin, so that they can worship the Father in Spirit and in truth and they will be able to serve God as acceptable in the spirit of holiness through the power of eternal life. This sanctification can only be accomplished by the power of the Holy Spirit that helps them to focus on their devotion to the truth revealed to them by the Spirit of Truth, which is the Living Word of God and the revelation of God.

All believers of Jesus Christ must sanctify themselves in order to receive the blessings of eternal life that comes to them only through Christ, their Savior Lord. After Jesus Christ had spoken the Word of God to His disciples, he also prayed for them. We can see it as a prayer after one sermon on a resurrection Sunday. Jesus Christ who only has the power of indwelling Spirit of Eternal Life called on God the Father and interceded in prayer, not only for the disciples, but to those of us today that believe in Him through the written Word of God in the Scriptures. We must let this also be our manner of service to the Lord after we have taught or preached to the congregation, the sinners and the lost. We must pray for them.

We must pray over the word that we preach so that God will put increase and apply it to the heart of men and women who hear it. Christ's disciples were now His family at that time because they have been together for a good three years. We should also see ourselves today as Christ's family. He is our Father in Heaven, our brother, our husbandman, our heavenly friend, our teacher, our preserver, our great intercessor in Heaven; moreover, He is our life. In Him, there is life, and life everlasting.

We should set a good example before the Master's families who blessed His household, and pray for them before leaving this Earth to Heaven where He continues to be our great intercessor. Christians must pray for their friends or for each other when they are parting or traveling from one end of the Earth to another; it is very good to depart with prayer. Christ's prayer was received before His sacrifice on the Cross, which he was about to offer on Earth at that time. Christ prayed then as a priest, which was about to offer sacrifices, in the character virtue of which all prayers were to be made. It was a prayer that was to be made; it was a prayer that was a sign of His intercession, which He ever lives to make for us within the veil.

Christ lifted up His eyes to Heaven, which most believers pray the same way today. This is a call to prayer with our hearts lifted up to Heaven. If God is our heavenly Father we have the liberty and confidence to approach Him, and with great expectation from Him. Jesus Christ's attributes of God the Father is that He has power over all what He has created in Heaven and on Earth below. The same power that the Father gave to the Son, which also is the power over all flesh. This is the foremost purpose of this power is the eternal life which the Father granted and designed by His power to those who believe in Jesus Christ.

Jesus Christ prayed for eternal life for those that the Father has given Him and to those the Father will still give Him until His Second Coming to this Earth. Thereby they have (the believers) been secured the happiness of eternal life. Eternal life can never die; it is an immortal crown that will never fade away. We have to praise and honor our Lord and Savior Jesus Christ for His gift of eternal life for those who believe in Him. The power of eternal life that Jesus Christ gave is incomprehensible and unattainable through any other means only in Jesus Christ who is the eternal life.

"One who has become a priest not on the basis of a regulation as to his ancestry but on the basis of the power of an indestructible life" (Hebrew 7:16). The Leviticus priesthood was imperfect and was administered by sinful humans. It was replaced by the perfect Priest, the Son of God. Christ is a perfect priest because he is wholly righteous, he provides a once and all sacrifice for our sins, he serves as our eternal priest before God in heaven and lives forever.

Therefore, our Lord and Savior Jesus Christ is able to save completely, and able to offer an indestructible life forever to all who come to God through Him. The High Priest of our profession holds His office by that innate power of endless life, which He has in Himself, to communicate eternal life to all those who duly rely, put their trust upon His sacrifice and intercession. "I know, O Lord, that man's life is not own; it is not for man to direct his steps" (Jeremiah 10:23). People of God are always under divine direction; in so much that they can only do what God permits them to do. Because He knows what is good for us and therefore controls the timing of our life if we put our trust in Him.

"For we are God's workmanship, created in Christ Jesus to do good works, which God prepared in advance for us to do" (Ephesians 2:10). Those who become new creatures in Jesus Christ receive continuing grace to live the Christian life where they resist sin, denounce it and all forms of sin and focus on the Lord earnestly seeking to serve Him and live for Him by His grace that works within them. The new man is a new creature, and God is the creator in Jesus Christ on the account of His atonement. God in His new creation has designed believers for good works and to do what is going to glorify His Holy name. "You, however, did not come to know Christ that way. Surely, you heard of Him and were taught in Him in accordance with the truth that is in Jesus. You were taught, with regard to your former way of life, to put off your old self, which is being corrupted by its deceitful desires; to be made new in the attitude of your minds; and to put on the new self, created to be like God in true righteousness and holiness" (Ephesians 4:20-24). All believers are united to Christ by faith and God dwells in all believers' hearts now, an eagerness of their dwelling together with Him to eternity.

Those who have learned from Christ are saved from the shadow of darkness, which other people in the world are still living. We must all learn from Jesus Christ. Christ is the greatest teacher in the universe. We are taught by Him and we live by His Word of life. Jesus Christ is the way, the truth and the life. Therefore, believers are taught the real truth by Christ Himself. Jesus Christ is our example both in doctrine and in His life.

The truth of Jesus Christ revealed in its beauty, power and love. Apostle Paul explains to us that the old man corrupted by sin must be put away. New believers in Christ must put on new nature as a new creature in that they will produce, by God's power, that looks and craves for God's good desire that will bring glory to Him, speaking truth with love. "No one has ever seen God, but God the Son and only, who is at the Father's side, has made Him known" (John 1:18). Salvation comes by the power of the Holy Spirit. Jesus Christ comes into our lives to regenerate our spirit and to recreate us in Christ's image. Christ's humanity and deity are united in Christ; Jesus is the eternal God; He became a human being.

CHAPTER FIVE

ETERNAL LIFE FROM EARTH TO HEAVEN

There is no one on this Earth that can have eternal life without receiving Jesus Christ as Lord and Savior. People of this Earth cannot know God without eternal life through Jesus Christ. Eternal life is given to those who have made Jesus their Lord and Savior. The Scripture has said it again and again that if you have Jesus Christ as your Lord and you will have eternal life. "No one can serve two masters." Our Lord Jesus Christ exposes those who put their own souls and trust in money along with material things of this world. They think that they can divide between God and the world to please God and please man too.

Either he will hate the one and love the other, or he will be devoted to the one and despise the other. You cannot serve both God and Money" (Matthew 6:24). The Scripture is telling us that to serve money is to place such a high value on it in so much that we place our trust and faith in it. Believers must not look, or handle it as if it is their ultimate security and happiness to the point that we expect it to guarantee our future, and our heart desire, more than we desire God's righteousness and kingdom from this when Jesus Christ becomes our Lord and Savior. He is the Lord of all: our wealth, our medical needs, and our entire life.

Jesus Christ does not say that people are not to make provisions for future physical needs. What He does forbid is the anxiety or worry that shows a lack or that can lead to lack, or weakness of faith in God's fatherly care and love. He wants us to live eternal life from this Earth to Heaven by completely putting all our lives in His Holy hands. He is powerful enough to take care of our finances.

"What shall we say, then, shall we go on sinning so that grace may increase? By no means! We died to sin; how can we live in it any longer? Or don't you know that all of us who were baptized into Christ Jesus were baptized into his death? We were therefore buried with him through baptism into death in order that, just as Christ was raised from the dead through the glory of the Father, we too may live a new life" (Romance 6:1-4). Apostle Paul challenges the believers concerning a new life in Christ. We see that true believers being in Christ, by virtue or through the baptism into Christ and into His death, so that their old life of sin is buried, moreover, believer have been translated from the sin nature into a new life in Christ. Because true believers have died to sin and therefore, made a definitive separation from their past life of sin, they will no longer continue in sin. If they continue to live in sin they are not converted and not a true believer of Jesus Christ.

Sin is also a moral corruption in human history that opposes all better human intentions. It causes people to commit unrighteousness with delight and to take pleasure in the evil actions of others. It is also a power that enslaves and corrupts, sin is rooted human desire. Sin was brought into the human race through Adam and Eve which affected every one as a result of the divine judgment that brought physical and spiritual death, and only be erase through the power of faith in Jesus Christ, His redemptive work on the Cross and the Holy Spirit.

Therefore, the water baptism for the Christian represents his or her burial and resurrection with Jesus Christ, accompanied with true faith. Jesus Christ, as a result of the believer's life in Him, is continuously flowing, pouring abundant grace and divine life to the believers.

This is the only way a believer is able to live and enjoy eternal life from this Earth to Heaven.

Baptism means identifying with Jesus Christ in His death and burial in order that we may live in union with His resurrected life. Jesus Christ rose from the dead, and all those who believe in Him will walk in newness of life. Apostle Paul says that those things that bring sin into our lives, any thought of countenance to sin are to be denounced and rejected in the areas of believer's lives. Believers must be seeking those things that will bring Holy Living, Holy Characters, and a new life. Believers must not only cease from any form of acts of sin, but he or she must get rid of any habits and any indications that weakened, or destroyed the body and soul; they must not encourage any habits to sin.

Christians must pursue holiness and righteousness from this Earth to Heaven. Believers must live a sacrificial life, dedicating themselves into what is pleasing and justifying in the eye of God, and be ready to serve Him faithfully and truthfully. Baptism binds, or glues believers to Jesus Christ. Baptism signifies and seals our union with Christ, so that we have nothing to do with sin anymore; we are complete, we are sealed to be the Lord's possessions. Therefore, a life devoted to God is a new life.

"Behold I will create new heavens and a new earth. The former things will not be remembered nor will they come to mind" (Isaiah 5:17). We should also look at, "As the new heaves and the new earth that I make will endure before me, declares the Lord, so will your name and descendants endure" (Isaiah 66:22). The word of the Lord came to Prophet Isaiah. God revealed to him that at the end of this age, the Messianic Kingdom age, God will create the new Heaven and the new Earth. There, all the believers of Jesus Christ will be with Him forever. This prophecy refers to God's future Kingdom on Earth. Prophet Isaiah blends the year of eternity where sin and death will be no more and unrighteousness will be no more.

Through the gift of grace, which believers have in and from Jesus Christ, we believers are to look for the new Heaven and the new Earth. Those who are in Christ are new creatures. This is a mighty, unspeakable happy change in the life of all believers. God reconciled believers, which gives them a new Heaven, which means creatures are reconciled to the believers, which also gives the believer a new Earth. All the believers through Jesus Christ shall be satisfied with life, in any circumstances of life. "Now we know that if the earthly tent we live in is destroyed, we have a building from God, an eternal house in heaven, not built by human hands" (2nd Corinthians 5:1). We have to know that the "tent" refers to the believer's earthly body, where there is a building of God eternal house in Heaven that will never be destroyed or decay, because it was not built by human hands. We live in a temporary body that is prepared while waiting for the resurrection of all the believers, which exist as disembodied spirit and naked soul without form.

Souls in Heaven wear white robes and are described as being visible just as Moses and Elijah appeared to Jesus Christ on the day of transfiguration; the same is for all the believers today. Since we do not know the time or hour of our Lord's return, believers have a powerful motivation for continual Holy Living. Believers know that they have a building of God; we have a firm foundation of expectation of the future in our Father's house and our everlasting home. It is our eternal house in the Heavens; like the earthly tabernacle the poor small house made with clay in which our souls now live. Those who belong to the Lord Jesus Christ, the people that have a walk with the Lord and give their lives to Him shall dwell forever with God.

The believer's assurance of the future blessedness, from the grace of God, making them to meet and receive this blessedness, all who are designed for Heaven hereafter, the spiritual building above are squared and fashioned here below. No other hand, less than the hand of God, can work in believers the things that the Spirit gave them assurance. "But in keeping with this promise we are looking forward to a new heaven and a new earth, the home of righteousness" (2nd Peter 3:13).

All the believers of Jesus Christ must eagerly hope for and earnestly expect the coming of the Lord. In the new Heaven and the new Earth everything is going to be as God wanted it to be; it is a way that only the righteous people lives. Believers must be in the state of reconciliation with God through Jesus Christ, focusing on and finding peace with God in our own consciences, as well as finding peace with man is a progressive pursuit that believers shall embrace; therefore, only the diligent, faithful Christian who will be happy in the day of our Lord and Savior will be rewarded. Jesus Christ will reward believers that diligently seek Him in the work He has assigned for them.

Believers must be living a life of purity, holiness and praise. "And this is what he promised as even eternal life" (1st John 2:25). Believers will remain in Christ and experience salvation only as long as they remain in the Word of God's teaching, remain in Christ and remain in the apostle. It is the truth of Christ that abides with believers that will help them to stay away from sin and it is the same truth that will secure the promise of eternal life. This promise that God the Father makes to His faithful believers with eternal life is what He only gives and to no one else. True believers of Jesus Christ have an inward confirmation of the divine truth. They have inhabitation of divine guidance through communion with the Lord and the Holy Spirit as they continue to follow the path of discipleship as a believer of Jesus Christ.

"Then I saw a new heaven and a new earth, for the first heaven and the first earth had passed away, and there was no longer any sea" (Revelation 21:1). The biblical interpretation of this verse is that the redeemed of God are a new creature transformed and redeemed in the world where Jesus Christ lives with His people and righteousness dwells in holiness and perfection. The new Earth will become the dwelling place of both humans and God.

All the redeemed will possess bodies like Christ's resurrection body (ones that are real, visible and tangible), but incorruptible and immortal. The New Jerusalem, which is already stationed in Heaven, will soon come down to Earth as the city of God for which Abraham and all the faithful people of God are waiting for and of which God is the architect and builder. The new Earth will become God's dwelling place, and He will remain with His people forever.

I AM THE ETERNAL LIFE

CHAPTER SIX

ETERNAL LIFE THAT THEY MAY KNOW YOU AS THE ONLY TRUE GOD

"Now this is eternal life that they may know you, the only true God, and Jesus, Whom you have sent" (John 17:3). This was Christ's priestly prayer for the disciples and for all those who believed in Him and had faith in Him. Eternal life is more than an endless existence. It is a special quality of life that believers receive when they partake of the essential life of God through Jesus Christ. This allows the believer of Jesus Christ to know God the Father in a growing, progressive knowledge and with intimate relationship with the Father, Son and the Holy Spirit. The present possession of eternal life requires a living faith in the Son; eternal life is a security that believers maintain by act of repentance asking for forgiveness of past, present and future sins.

It also involves present living on Earth with obedience and union with Him in everything we do, making Him the Lord and Savior of our lives. Maintaining a continual relationship with Jesus Christ who is the author and finisher of our faith should be of utmost importance. Eternal life associated with coming to Jesus Christ by faith, living a life of faith in Christ's finished work of redemption. Living by faith and by the power of the indwelling of the Holy Spirit.

"Therefore, brothers, we have an obligation but it is not the sinful nature, to live according to it. For if you live according to the sinful nature, you will die but if by the Spirit you put to death the misdeeds of the body, you will live, because those who are led by the Spirit of God are Sons of God" (Romans 8:12-14). Jesus Christ came to give us life here and now. The Holy Spirit, who raised Jesus from the dead, desires to impart life even to our mortal bodies, as we embrace His life with us, the Holy Spirit is the Spirit of Life in Christ Jesus.

Jesus Christ prayed for the protection, joy, sanctification, love and unity for His people who abide in Him. He prayed for those who believed and belonged to

God: believers of Jesus Christ who are separated from the world, who obey the Word of God and who accepted Jesus Christ's teaching and preaching. This is the great work Jesus has done for the believer's salvation. He brings all those who believe in Him to receive eternal life that they may know the true God, God the Father Almighty, Jesus Christ His only begotten Son and Holy Spirit ever as one God.

Since Jesus Christ spoke about eternal life both ways, it is both a future blessing and present possession. As we come to know God, the Father, God the Son and God the Holy Spirit we begin to experience the blessings of eternal life. Knowing God and Jesus Christ goes beyond human knowledge; it implies an active relationship between God the Father and God the Son. It also implies a progressive knowledge and understanding, which can only come by an active relationship with Jesus Christ. This is the only way to the Father or to know God the Father and to joyfully acknowledge His sovereignty. Believers must great receive the acceptance of His love, mercy and moreover, His intimate relationship with Jesus Christ through the Word of God that lives and abides forever to us and from us through our prayers.

The greatest end which the Christian religion set forward before believers is eternal life. Christ reveals eternal life to all those who believe in Him and He secures all those that the Father gave Him. Eternal life lies in the knowledge of God and Jesus Christ. Those that are brought in union with Christ and live a life of communion with God in Christ find the knowledge of God to be peaceful and joyful as Christ leads them in eternal life. Jesus Christ prays significantly for the believers. Christ is glorified in the believers through God the Father, and Christ glorified all the believers through God the Father.

Believers who are full of faith and are in the relationship between the Father and the Son whereby God the Father glorified the Son. This prayer of Christ still fills believers up until today. Jesus Christ glorified the Father by His sinless life, by His miracles, by His suffering, by His death on the Cross and by His resurrection. Christ finished the work of redemption for our salvation that the Father had given Him. The work of redemption of Jesus Christ brought glory to the Father; it glorified the Father's great wisdom in the redemptive work of humanity. Christ's redemptive work glorified the faithfulness, holiness and love of God the Father.

It showed that God is the immortal, the invisible, the all-wise God whom is providence that is unsearchable, a just God and justifier of those who do not believe in Him. Jesus Christ works of redemption shows that he is the only God who promised and fulfilled; He fulfilled His promises for Abraham, Isaac and Jacob. God the Father is a God of promise; He is the promisor of those who diligently seek Him. Right from the Book of Genesis to the Book of Revelation, Jesus Christ's work of redemption shows, acknowledges and proves that God the Father's love by sending Jesus as the mediator of a New Covenant and co-eternal with His Son, Jesus Christ. Likewise, the redemptive work of Jesus Christ on the Cross brought glory to Him as the true Son of God full of grace and truth. It glorified His passion for sinners. His patience was also glorified in the power to save and redeem those who believe in Him.

The work of redemption of Jesus Christ showed Him as the most compassionate incarnate Son of God that came to this Earth and died, offering Himself as a sacrifice for our sins on the Cross. Christ bought our redemption with His precious blood. The redemptive work of Christ brought glory to the Son because He willingly submitted Himself for an atoning sacrifice for our sins and the sins of the whole people on Earth. The work of redemption glorified Jesus Christ and displayed that He is the most powerful man on Earth by bearing the weight of all the transgressions of the people in the world and destroying the works of Satan.

This is the reason why Jesus Christ our Lord and Savior prayed, "Glorify me in your presence with the glory I had with you before the world begun" (John 17:24). Our Lord wants the Father to restore Him back to his original glory, which He shared with the Father before the incarnation was resumed. This clearly proves the pre-existence of Christ with the Father where He dwelt in Heaven with the Father before e came to the world.

CHAPTER SEVEN

ETERNAL LIFE THE JOY OF THE BELIEVERS

"And the God of all grace, who called you to his eternal glory in Christ, after you have suffered a little while, will himself, restore you and make you strong, firm and steadfast" (1st Peter 5:10). The joy of the believer of Jesus Christ comes with true victory in persecution, afflictions and trouble seen by God working with us behind the scenes, performing His wonderful power of love in our lives. In everything we might be going through we should always remember that He is the God of all grace. This demonstrates to us that God deals with us according to His riches in glory, not based on what we deserve, but on His thoughts of His infinite love for the believers. No matter how difficult our testing and trials may be, believers must be thankful.

The joy of believer's eternal life is also in our consolation that we have to remember that God calls us to His eternal glory in Christ Jesus; it enables us to look beyond our sufferings of this life, but focus on Jesus Christ our Savior and be like Him forever in eternity. Believers must also rejoice because their suffering is temporary. We must be encouraged that God uses suffering to teach us, mold us and to be people of good Christian character. In trials God makes believer fit and strong; He supplies all that we need to go through all the trials we face in life and makes us spiritually matured to be what He wants us to be for His glory.

Suffering also makes believers more stable as believers are able to maintain good confession, to be strong under pressure and to be strengthened in spirit, soul and body. The enemy uses persecution, troubles and afflictions to discourage believers; it does not have any effect because Christ is the hope of glory of the believer. He strengthens them to endure and persevere under trial.

The joy of eternal life always yields a blessed result in the believer's character, refining the faith, adjusting the character, establishing, strengthening and settling with a sound foundation. God wants every believer to be firmly planted and secured in a place where Jesus Christ's Word flows into believer as the water flows. Apostle Peter prayed that God would perfect His good work that He started in the life of every believer. Those who are called to be joint heirs of eternal life through Jesus Christ must suffer in this world, but their sufferings will be for a little time.

Believers must depend upon God's promises; He will fulfill His promise. In a miraculous way God will take care of all our persecution, afflictions and troubles so that we can be able to worship Him with the Spirit of holiness. We can see the eternal life joy of the believer in the Old Testament Scripture, "You have made known to me the path of life; you will fill me with joy in your presence" (Psalm 16:11). Believers must have confidence in the Lord that He will show us the path of life so that we can be able to serve Him better.

This path of life will lead every believer straight to Heaven. This verse is particularly David's prophetic word of Christ; he was carried away by the spirit in the holy elevations towards God before the glory of Messiah. This verse applies to all the believers of Jesus Christ because Christ is the head of the Church. The joy of eternal life of believers is found in, "But the Spirit is love, joy, peace, patience, kindness, goodness, faithfulness, gentleness and self-control, against such things there is no law" (Galatians 5:22). The best joy of the eternal life is the fruit of the Spirit. Believers must be filled with all the fruits of the Holy Spirit; they must allow the Holy Spirit to produce all the fruits of the Spirit within them.

Christ commends believers with love; the joy by which we may delight in the Lord, peace with God, bear more and more peaceable fruits to other people around us. The joy of eternal life is the new life and the new character of believers after we receive eternal life. We must exercise faith, meekness, goodness and readiness to do good to all as we have the opportunity to do so, not to be easily angered, but promote what is good. Thus to crucify the flesh and not to fulfill it's lustful desires, this is what the believer must be - pure and holy at all times.

CHAPTER EIGHT

JESUS CHRIST: THE SOURCE OF ETERNAL LIFE

Jesus Christ is the source of eternal life. He died on the Cross to save all those who come to Him and He lives to keep all those who believe in Him to the end. We love Jesus because He loved us first. Jesus Christ, the only begotten incarnate Son of the Father, full of grace and truth, He is the only source of eternal life because He is the eternal life.

"For God did not send his Son into the world to condemn the world, but to save the world through him. Whoever believes in him is not condemned, but whoever does not believe stands condemned already because he has not believed in the name of God's one and only Son" (John 17:18). We have to be fully assured that Jesus Christ is the source, the only source of eternal life as He is the only Son of God that the Father sent to the world.

There are so many convictions that Jesus Christ is God's Son and the only Savior of the universe. He surrendered Himself with obedience to the Father. Believers must be willingly to surrender their life to Jesus Christ. They must fully trust with strong faith in Jesus Christ and rest assured that He is both able and willing to bring all believers to final salvation and into a close communion with God the Father in Heaven. God the Father does not want anyone to perish; He bestows the gift of eternal life to anyone who puts his or her trust in Jesus Christ, His only begotten Son.

Eternal life is a life that frees believer from the power of Satan and places them in the hand of God. This is a great mystery, which was revealed in the Gospel of John. Now we know that God loves the people that He created by giving His only begotten Son for atonement for our sins. In order to permanently complete the work of redemption once and for all, God the Father sacrificed His own Son for the salvation of the human race.

Through Jesus Christ, who is the source of eternal life all the people of this world, has been offered the gift of grace no matter who you are and what your religion, either

Jewish and Gentiles, to include all other people of so many religions, Christ is the only way to Heaven, the only source of eternal life. Through Christ Jesus, God took our sins away and He sees Christ's righteousness in the believers. God has taken away the believer's sins; they cannot die, they will have eternal life forever lives in Christ and God the Father.

They are entitled to all the joy of Heaven; they shall possess eternal life everlasting life. Jesus Christ is the resurrection, "I am the resurrection and the life. He who believes in me will live, even though he dies, and who ever lives and believes in me will never die. Do you believe this?" (John 11:25-26). Jesus Christ is the God of resurrection and the life. People that believe in Jesus Christ made Him their Lord and Savior; physical death is not a tragic end. Instead, it is a get way to abundant eternal life and communion with God.

Jesus Christ said those who believe in Him will live forever. He is referring to the power of the resurrection; and when He said they will never die means that the believers resurrected body and soul will never cease to exist. They will also have new bodies, which will be immortal, imperishable, incorruptible that can never die or deteriorate, perfectly designed by God for the higher life to come, or higher Heaven hereafter.

"I tell you the truth," Jesus replied, "No one who has left home or brothers or sisters or mother or father or children or fields for me and the gospel will fail to receive a hundred times as much in this present age (homes, brothers, sisters, mothers, children and fields –and with them persecutions) and in the age to come eternal life. But many who are first will be last, and the last first" (Mark 10:29-31). Jesus Christ was explaining to the disciples how great the rewards promised by the Father. The blessings and the inheritance joy in the relationships with Christ will be experience by the true believers who sacrifice themselves for Christ's sake to enhance the work of the kingdom of God.

Eternal life is promised by Christ and He is the source of eternal life. He will fulfill His promise to all who believe in Him. Jesus Christ reconciled the apostles and His disciples by referring them to the mighty power of God that will help each individual, no matter who they are, rich and poor, to prevail over all the difficulties that they will go through in the cause of their salvation. The greatest of the salvation of those that are rich in this world is very little and should be left alone for Jesus Christ.

Jesus Christ reassured His disciples, including us as today's believers, that not only will they be recompensed, or shall be reimbursed, those who have left either little things or great things, any worldly wealth, they must know to receive Christ and eternal life is the best thing that can happen to people in this world; the greatest gift of salvation is worth more than rubies and gold and all the worldly wealth.

They must remember that they stand nearer to Christ then any creature. The greatest trial of a believer is when His love for Jess Christ comes to stand as a competition with the worldly wealth. Believers must forsake so many things in order to be fully in Christ. Jesus Christ will abundantly reward any believer that loves Him sincerely and does His will. They shall have eternal life and receive a hundred fold in this world, what people cannot even imagine. Living for Christ is the best thing that can happen to the people of this world; it is a life full of contentment and joy. It is a life that communicates with God and is close to Him; it is a life of prayer and a life of hope of eternal life, which the Lord promised.

Believers must be living in humble obedience to the will of God. They must make Christ to become the author of their eternal salvation, which means eternal life that is bestowed only on all who believe and obey the commandment of Jesus Christ. Believers must hearken to His Word with the spirit of obedience.

CHAPTER NINE

ETERNAL LIFE ENCOURAGEMENT TO BELIEVERS

"May our Lord Jesus Christ himself and God our Father, who loved us and by his grace gave us eternal encouragement and good life" (2nd Thessalonians 2:16). Apostle Paul encouraged all the believers of Jesus Christ and prays his prayer for them, which continues up until today. He lets us know that eternal life is a great gift from God the Father, God the Son, and God the Holy Spirit, the Holy Trinity forever as one God. God revealing the glory of Christ is more than His sublime majesty and the manifestation of the radiance of His power, which existed before the creation of the world.

It is all that Christ is in His power, character and authority, which includes His love, holiness, righteousness, mercy, grace and truth. His glory is the radiance of all that He is as the God of resurrection. "Therefore, the holy brothers, who share in the heavenly calling, fix your thoughts on Jesus, the apostle and high priest whom we confess" (Hebrew 1:3). This verse was addressed to Old Testament people of God such as those who are under the Old Testament covenant. Moses was sent by God. He was an apostle and Aaron was the high priest in the old covenant of God. The apostle of Jesus Christ is under the New Testament and New Covenant where these two offices of the covenant of God's order were combined into one with the person of Jesus Christ.

It is also applies to today's believers, both Jewish Christians of Paul's day, as well as the Gentile Christians of today. Believers after their conversion were immediately exposed to persecution, afflictions and a lot of various things that could cause discouragement, basically anything that caused them to drift away from salvation. But if believers continue to hold onto Jesus Christ and God's grace, this will make possible our saving relationship in Christ and in His redeeming grace, which is more than sufficient to sustain us in all trials and tribulations. The believer's eternal security will be maintained as they remain loyal to Christ and thus do not abandon their faith in a loving obedience to Him.

The love of God is the spring and fountain of all the good we have and hope for; from this fountain all our consolation flows through us and to others who did not believe and make them to believe. The consolation of all the believers is an everlasting consolation. The comfort of the believer of Jesus Christ is not a dying faith. The believers consolation is founded on the hope of the eternal life through the grace and mercy of God, Believers' hope remains and maintains strong and in stability, hope for what is unseen, but founded in the eternal life.

Believers of Jesus Christ must pray without ceasing for the success of the Gospel ministry around the world. Pray that the Word of God might get ground, that the Gospel may have free course to the hearts and the consciences of the people of this world, and that it may be glorified; in the conversion of the soul of sinners. For God to continuously spread the glory the Gospel and by so doing, be glorifying Himself and His Holy name and the people of the world will turn to Him and give Him glory that is due Him. Believers must be established in every good word and work. Jesus Christ must be honored by our good works and words. This is the eternal life encouragement of the believers of Jesus Christ to be one in Him as he and Father are one.

CHAPTER TEN

ETERNAL GLORY

"For our light and momentary troubles are achieving for us an eternal glory that far outweighs them all. So we fix our eyes not on what is seen, but on what is unseen. For what is seen is temporary, but what is unseen is eternal" (2nd Corinthians 4:17.) The hardships endured in the lives of those who remain faithful to Jesus Christ are light in comparison to the abundance of glory we have through Christ. This glory is already present with the believers in part, but will be fully experienced in the future when believers reach their heavenly inheritance; we will say that the severest tribulations were nothing compared with the glory of the eternal state. Therefore, believers must not lose hope or give up their faith as they are going through earthly problems.

Believers must pray for the renewal of their innermost soul, every day as long as they live on this Earth. Just as in a non-believer the thoughts of evil increase in them every day and move them far away from God, and the things of God. It is the same way for believers who are godly people. They grow better and better inwardly every day and closer and closer to Christ every day receiving the life of Christ and eating the Bread of Life and drinking the water of life that wells up in them to the life eternal.

The prospect of eternal life and the happiness of new life in Christ kept them from falling and from fainting when facing any earthly troubles and tribulations. Christian believers found afflictions to be light, afflictions makes them look at the Heaven and the glory of the Lord that is waiting for them. The glory of Heaven was to be far more exceeding than what they were going through on Earth.

Faith in Christ, Christ only perceived to be light and short, but for a moment. The believers' faith enabled them to make this right judgment of things around them; unseen things are eternal, what we see is temporal, by faith the believer not only discerns good things, what is coming to pass, and the great difference between them, but by this also we take our aim at unseen things, which is eternal life in the heavens.

The believer's assurance of the future blessedness from the experience of the grace of God will make them for this blessedness. All who are designated, designed and prepared for Heaven while they were still here on Earth being the stones of that spiritual building above are squared and fashioned here below. They live heavenly life while they are still here on Earth. Even though they are still on Earth, they are at the same time present with the Lord in spirit.

"Consider that our present sufferings are not worth comparing with the glory that will be revealed in us" (Romans 8:18) The Scripture is telling us that all the earthly sufferings of this present world such as sickness, pain, misery, disappointments, poverty, mistreatment, sorrow, persecution and all various kinds of trouble that the believers are going through must be considered insignificant when compared with the blessings, privileges and glory that will be given to the faithful believers in the world to come.

A true believer's reward shall be an inheritance. Those that now partake of the Spirit of Christ, as His brethren, shall partake of His glory. Those true believers that suffer with Christ shall be glorified with Him. "Therefore, I endure everything for the sake of the elect that they too may obtain the salvation that is in Christ Jesus, with eternal glory." (2nd Timothy 2:10). Believers are like soldiers, they must be willing to undergo difficulties and suffering and to wage spiritual warfare in wholehearted devotion to their Lord and Savior Jesus Christ.

Believers are like an athlete; they must be willing to strive for the gold medal for Christ, willing to sacrifice all things, their possessions, positions, family and live lives of discipline. Believers must discipline themselves in order to win souls for Christ, and in order to be fully used for the service of the Lord. Like a farmer, they must be patient in seed sowing and committed to hard work with long hours. Jesus Christ will carry out both His promises to His people. Divine faithfulness is a comfort for those who remain loyal and God will faithfully fulfill His word and promise. Believers should be willing to do great things for the salvation of sinners' souls, suffer anything in order to promote the salvation of all the people in the world.

Apostle Paul encourages Timothy, as well as encouraged all the believers of Jesus Christ today.

Believers must grow stronger and stronger in their pursuit of which is good. Jesus Christ's grace is all-sufficient and like blessings of eternal glory is awaiting believers.

I AM THE ETERNAL LIFE

CHAPTER ELEVEN

ASSURANCE OF ETERNAL LIFE

"Now there is in store for me the crown of righteousness, which the Lord, the righteous Judge, will award to me on that day and not only to me, but also to all who have longed for his appearing" (2nd Timothy 4:8). Apostle Paul remains faithful to the Lord in the service of the Lord and in everything that pertains to the Gospel of God. He was able to say boldly and confidently that a crown of righteousness is awaiting him. We believers of Jesus Christ must be faithful and diligent in the service of the Lord so that we can be able as Apostle Paul said that crown of righteousness is awaiting us. We must remain faithful to our Lord and Savior and the Gospel of God that entrusted to us the spirit of witnessing. Clearly Apostle Paul knew that God's loving approval and crown was waiting for him in Heaven. In the same way we believers of today must work hard and gain the approval of the indwelling of the Spirit of God that will say clearly a reward and crown is waiting for us in Heaven.

God has reserved many, many rewards according to our service on Earth to Him in Heaven for all those who remain loyal and faithful to Christ Jesus and His gospel. "For we must all appear before the judgment seat of Christ, that each one may receive what is due him for the things done while in the body, whether good or bad" (2nd Corinthian 5:10). We must fight this good fight; we must fight it out, and finish our course towards the end of our days to be able to speak in a manner that will offer comfort to others. We must let this word of Apostle Paul to Timothy encourage us to endure hardness as a good soldier of Jesus Christ that there is a crown of life waiting for us in Heaven.

Heaven is where our holiness and righteousness will be perfected, and our crown will be worn. This crown of believers that is awaiting them, that already is laid up for them, they have it not in their possession, but it is like a treasure, money in the bank for believers which cannot fade away or be destroyed. Most importantly, it can neither be devalued. It is a blessed assurance when Jesus is yours and you are in Jesus. Jesus Christ the great Judge before whose judgment seat we must appear, the Lord Jesus Christ; will recompense us for what He receives from us, for the things done in the body. All Christians must be persuaded, make it a matter of significant to respect and live a holy life, that God requires from all those who give their life to Him so that when Christ shall appear in the air to judge the people of this Earth they may appear before Him with confidence.

All Christians must be clear minded and of self-controlled. They must watch, as well pray without ceasing. They must live holy and godly lives. They must show mercy and kindness to all the people around them. They must allow the Holy Spirit to manifest in their lives, with a spirit of love, mercy and all the fruits of the spirit to be produced in their lives. The crown of righteousness and the crown of life are awaiting those who faithfully and sincerely serve the Lord in the Spirit of Holiness. The assurance of eternal life will be surely made manifest in their lives.

I AM THE ETERNAL LIFE

CHAPTER TWELVE

FROM EARTH TO LIFE ETTERNAL

"For every living soul belongs to me, the Father as well as the Son both alike belong to me. The soul who sins is the one who will die" (Ezekiel 18:4).

Children are affected by the sins of their parents; however, prophet Ezekiel makes it clear that these passages were not intended to teach that children were to be punished for their father's sins. All believers both father and mother will be accountable for their own sins and their own unwillingness to trust in Jesus Christ as their Savior Lord; and to live a righteous life that God required from them.

Apostle Paul stated and made it clear to all the believers in the Book of Romans where He restates the principles with Scriptures, "For the wages of sin is death, but the gift of God is eternal life in Christ Jesus our Lord" (Romans 6:23). A believer who has a right relationship with the Lord and who as well demonstrated that commitment to God, who therefore, loves righteousness and justice, it is this individual who will from this Earth eternally be in communion and favor with the Lord. Jesus Christ the maker of all things that consists in a particular manner; his the Father of Spirit for his image was stamped on the soul of human beings from the beginning of creation and He renovated the heart of men.

God bears a good will both to Father and Son, and will put no hardship upon any one. God is loving-kindness; He has great love and kindness for all the souls of humanity He created. He does not want any souls to die, but only when, through their own fault, they fall into sin. Sin is the activity of the soul, which means the punishment of sin is death. God sent His Son to the world to redeem us from sin and death to make us alive in Him through His righteousness. He wants us to live from this Earth to eternal life in Him. When God raised Jesus Christ from the dead, He automatically raised up all believers together with

Him; and placed Jesus Christ, His Son, at His right hand in the heavenly places. God advanced and glorified all the believers in Him with Him. All the believers will live a blessed eternal life, lives from this Earth to Heaven, while sinners are rolling themselves in the dust; believer's sanctifying souls will sit in heavenly places with Christ. The world and all the material things of this world is nothing to them, compared with what has been designed and compared with the world of sin. Believers were exalted to reign with Christ in Heaven; they will sit upon the throne with Jesus Christ. "For it is by grace you have been saved, through faith and this not from yourselves, it is the gift of God not by works, so that no one can boast. For we are god's workmanship, created in Christ Jesus to do good works, which God prepared in advance for us to do" (Ephesians 2:8-10). There is no one that can be saved by works, good deeds of love, or any type of efforts in order to keep God's commandments. One must therefore be saved by the grace of God.

The grace of God is the eternal life, which is in Christ Jesus our Lord. The reasons for this are the following: All the unsaved people in the world are spiritually dead. They are under Satan's rule and dominion, and are surely enslaved to sin. They possess the sin nature and they are under God's condemnation. In order to live on this Earth and gain eternal life people must be saved, they must receive God's provision of salvation. He has forgiven them of their sin and they must be made spiritually alive. That means they must be delivered from the power of Satan and sin. They must be made a new creation from this Earth and receive the Holy Spirit who will dwell in them and make them live a holy and godly life from this Earth in order to be qualified for eternal life when their life here on Earth has ended.

"And this is what he promised us even eternal life" (1st John 2:25). Believers must be able to remain in Christ throughout their life on Earth immediately after conversion in order to experience salvation, which can only be achieved as long as they remain in the original teaching of Christ and the Apostles. Therefore, it is very important for all the believers to study the Scripture, eat it as food, and drink the word of God as if they are drinking water, until they hold firmly to Jesus Christ and His redeeming power and to God's word which abides and lives forever.

Every soul of every believer depends on this truth with the Word of God help the Holy Spirit to be active in the lives of believers of Jesus Christ. The word of God helps the soul to reach the eternal destinies of every believer and their lives on Earth depend on the Word of God. The Word of God will make them spiritually alive to receive the eternal life. Apostle advises the disciples and all the believers today to continue in the truth of the Word of God that was first communicated to them.

The truth concerning Jesus Christ that was delivered to them from the beginning must not be exchanged. Many pastors preach a wrong Gospel today. They changed from what the Word of God in the Bible says. They twisted the Word of God to suit their own purpose and to what their congregation want to hear. They are making congregations in thousands, upon thousands, but they are not making disciples or converting souls into the hands of the Lord. The true believers will receive by their faith and truth to the Word of God; they will continue to maintain holy union with God and Jesus Christ. Jesus Christ will continue to abide in believers that cleanse themselves from their sins through the power of the Holy Spirit, which unites them to the Son of God Jesus Christ. Believers will thereby, secure the promise of eternal life. Great is the promise of eternal life that God promised and fulfills to those who love His appearing of His Son Jesus Christ.

I AM THE ETERNAL LIFE

CHAPTER THIRTEEN

GIFT OF ETERNAL LIFE

"To those who by persistence in doing good seek glory, honor, and immortality, he will give eternal life" (Romans 2:7).

In the very beginning Jesus Christ promised believers the gift of eternal life that is why he said, "I am the eternal life" (John 17:3 *emphasis is mine*). Apostle Paul clearly states this fundamental truth concerning God's dealing with the entire people of the world. He let them know and made it clear to them that God punishes evildoers and rewards the righteous. The righteous are those who have been justified by faith and have peace with God. They are those who persevere in doing what is right according to God's standard. These are the believers that value highly the glory that comes from the Father of light.

They seek eternal life; those who seek the immortality do so by grace through faith. They are faithful believers that enter into God's glory, honor and immortality by their persistence in doing good through the power of the Holy Spirit that indwells them through the enabling of grace given to them by Jesus Christ. While those who do evil are those who are selfish, disobedient to the truth of the Word of God, and take pleasure in unrighteousness, in immoral lives, in wickedness. They will receive trouble, distress and the wrath of God. All who continue in sin will also perish, even though they have the knowledge of God's law, God's words, God's commandment, but they continue to live lives of sin. They take pleasure in worldly lust, which ruins the soul.

They have the measure of wrong and right. God will not automatically save those who do not hear the Gospel, nor will he give them a second chance after death. They will face eternal consequences for their actions. Apostle Paul urges all the Christians to be obedient, hearing the Word of God from the pastors avails nothing apart from faith, submission and obedience. Believers must be obedient; this obedience comes from faith, which is expressing itself through the love of Christ. There is a holy character in every religion. Those whom the righteous God will reward first are those true believers who fix and focus themselves to the right thing in life. These are the believers that desire and aim as high as the heavens and they are very strong in the Lord and they will not take no for an answer. They focus a hundred percent of their attention on how to live for the glory of the Lord.

    They are one in Christ as Christ is one with the Father. They are very firm in their foundation as the people of God and they live their life to the glory of God the Father, Son and Holy Spirit. They patiently wait on the promise of the Lord, not only in the length of their service for the Lord, but in all the difficulty they were going through in the cause of their service of the Lord's work. They continue to put on a great deal of patience in order to persevere. God will surely bless them and confer to them the gift of eternal life. Heaven is life; eternal life is called and consisted of glory; honor and peace. The gift of eternal life is not only an infinite life, but also an eternal quality of life, which helps the believer to maintain an intimate relationship with Jesus Christ; whereby, Christ's life and His divine nature is placed in every believer and every believer is in Him. Christ is the gift of eternal life; to be in Christ is to receive the gift of eternal life.

The gift of eternal life begins at the second birth when those who were dead in their sins and transgressions are made alive in Christ after receiving the gift of eternal life. Eternal life's gift is everlasting because the very life of Jesus Christ has been imparted to all those who believed in Him and to all those who made Him their Lord and Savior. The moment believers received the gift of grace of the salvation of God, the Holy Spirit abide in the heart of the believer helps him to live a life that he or she will receive the gift of eternal life from this Earth to Heaven.

"Who is a deposit guaranteeing our inheritance until the redemption of those who are God's possession to the praise of his glory" (Ephesians 1:14). God the Father Almighty chose in Jesus Christ people whom He has destined to be holy and blameless in His sight. God decided before the creation of the universe those who will receive the gift of eternal life through His Son Jesus Christ.

The election to salvation and holiness of the body of Christ is always certain. But the certainty for the individual believers remains conditional, which is based on their own personal living faith in Jesus Christ and also their perseverance in union with Him. "He did not enter by means of the blood of goats and calves; but he entered the Most Holy place once for all by his own blood, having obtained eternal redemption. The blood of goats and bulls and the ashes of a heifer sprinkled on those who are ceremonially unclean sanctify them so that they are outwardly clean. How much more, then, will the blood of Christ, who through the eternal Spirit offered himself unblemished to God, cleanse our consciences from acts that lead to death, so that we may serve the living God. For this reason Christ is the mediator of a new covenant, that those who are called may receive the promise of eternal inheritance now that he has died as a ransom to set them free from the sins committed under the first covenant" (Hebrew 9:12-15).

The blood of Jesus Christ is central to the concept of redemption. On the cross Jesus Christ shed His innocent blood in order to remove the sins of the people of this world, whether Jewish or Gentiles or other people of other religions, and to reconcile the people of the world with God. By Christ's blood, He accomplished the following: His blood forgives the sins of all who repent and believe in Him; His blood was ransoms all believers from the power of Satan and evil; His blood justifies all who believe in Him; His blood cleanses believers' consciences that they might serve God, without guilt in singleness of heart with full assurance of faith; His blood sanctifies God's people;

His Blood opens the way for believers to come directly to the Throne of grace, and before God through Him in order to find grace and that grace may abound in all the areas of their lives, as well as mercy to help in salvation. Christ's blood guarantees of all the promises of the New Covenant. The saving faith reconciling and purifying power of Jesus' blood continually appropriated to all the believers as they come to God through Christ. How wonderful and how powerful is the love of Christ to all those who believe in Him. The gift of eternal life is incomparable and incomprehensible. We have to praise Him continually with the fruit of our lips giving Him praises and thankfulness forever.

Jesus Christ offered Himself to God. Christ offered Himself to God through the eternal Spirit. It was Christ offering Himself to God without spot, without any sinful stain. The blood of Christ is sufficient to purge the conscience from dead works. It reaches to the bottom of the soul and conscience. It is sufficient to enable all the believers to serve the living God by sanctifying and renewing the believer's soul through the gracious influence of the Holy Spirit.

Jesus Christ, through the eternal Spirit and by the power of the indwelling of the Holy Spirit, helps those who believe in Him and put their faith and trust in him to receive the gift of eternal life from this Earth to Heaven.

I AM THE ETERNAL LIFE

CHAPTER FOURTEEN

FOREVER LIVE WITH GOD

"Surely goodness and love will follow me all he days of my life, and I will dwell in the house of the Lord forever" (Psalm 23:6).

This Psalm, conceived in the mind of the Lord and inspired by the Holy Spirit, it expresses the Lord's concern and diligent care for those who follow Him. Believers are in the cherished object of Christ's divine love. He cares for every individual person that the Father entrusted into His care because Christ is the Shepherd of the sheep. God the Father, God the Son and God the Holy Spirit compares Himself as a shepherd in order to explain His great love for the people of this world.

Our Lord Jesus Christ Himself expresses His relationship with the people of this world as a Savior of the world. God the Father Almighty through Jesus Christ and the Holy Spirit is so concerned about the people of this world and all His children that He desires to love, care for, protect, guide and He comes close near to the heart just as a good shepherd cares for his sheep. Believers belong to Jesus Christ as He is the Good Shepherd, the Great Shepherd and the Chief Shepherd of the sheep.

All Christians in the world are the Lord's sheep. They belong to Him and they are the special object of His affection and attention. We love Him because He loved us first, and He gave His life to us, that those who live and believe in Him should not live for themselves, but live for Him who loved them and gave His life to them as atonement for their sin. "We all, like sheep, have gone astray, each of us has turned to his own way; and the Lord has laid on him the iniquity of us all" (Isaiah 53:6). Prophet Isaiah was telling us that at one point of time or another every one that came to this Earth has preferred to follow his own selfish and sinful ambitions and they did not follow God's righteous command. They are all guilty; they were all in need of savior. Christ Jesus died in our place. God therefore, imputed the righteousness of Christ in those who believe in Him. When God sees us, He sees us through Jesus Christ. His blood atones for all our iniquities. The Lord has redeemed every believer with His shed blood on the Cross and we now belong to Him forever. Forever we will live with the Lord from here on Earth and when we get to Heaven. His righteousness becomes our righteousness. We are His sheep. We can claim the promises of God that eternally live with Christ forever when we respond to His voice and follow Him. With the Shepherd accompanying the sheep in this life's pilgrimage, believers will receive constant grace, help, kindness and divine support. No matter what happens to believers, they must continue to trust the Good Shepherd to work in all this for their good. The goal of all the believer is to follow the Good Shepherd and experiencing His goodness, mercy and love and hope that one day they will be with the Lord forever, behold his face and continue to serve Him forever in Heaven.

All the believers that seek Him are promised with blessings. Those who seek Him with clean hands and pure hearts which means their inward holiness with right motives will see the Lord and forever live with Him. Believers should remind themselves of this promise of God every time they call unto Him in prayer and supplication, believers must worship Him in His house or seek His grace in the Lord's supper, do what is pleasing and justifying in His sight, adoring Him and blessing His Holy name. Believers will look into Jesus as the One and only, the author and finisher of our faith.

Jesus Christ said, "I am the good shepherd" (John 10:11). Jesus Christ declares Himself to be the promised good shepherd that David wrote about in the Old Testament. This illustration shows Jesus' tender heart and devoted care for His people. This means He is toward all who believe in Him as a good shepherd is toward His sheep, caring, watching and loving them every minute. This emphasizes the uniqueness of Jesus Christ as the shepherd of the sheep; His death on the cross saves all his sheep.

"May the God of peace, who through the blood of eternal covenant brought back from the dead Our Lord Jesus, that great shepherd of the sheep equip you with everything good for doing his Will, and many he work in us what is pleasing to him, through Jesus Christ to whom be glory for ever and ever amen" (Hebrew 13:20-21). God is the God of peace because he planned the way for peace and reconciliation between Himself and the sinners. The great work of redemption was accomplished through our Lord and Savior Jesus Christ who Himself is the Prince of Peace. God is the God of peace by the divine power by which He raised our Lord Jesus from the dead. Our Lord Jesus Christ was called and the title was bestowed upon Him because he is the Savior of every soul of each human being on Earth and He is the Great Shepherd of the sheep.

Believers are the flocks of His pasture, and He cares and has concern for them. The blood of Christ is the sanction and seals of an everlasting covenant between God and His people, the believers. Jesus Christ is, "And when the chief shepherd appears, you will receive the crown of glory that will never face away" (1st Peter 5:4). God works in a miraculous way in the life of all the believers of Jesus Christ by the perfection of the believers in every good work. This is a greatly desired by believer and for the believers. Moreover, the way in which God makes His people perfect, it is by working in them through the power of the indwelling of the Holy Spirit that always help the believer to do what is pleasing in God's sight at all time. The Holy Spirit is the counselor, wonderful, the comforter, who reveals to us the Word of God, who teaches us the Word of God and makes known God's will for our lives.

Jesus Christ is the Chief Shepherd of the flocks in the world and the heritage of God. Christ is the Chief

Shepherd over all inferior shepherds; the Chief Shepherd will appear to judge all the people of the world. Those that are found to faithfully serve the Lord in their duty will receive from the Chief Shepherd a crown of glory that faded not away. Poor and dispersed suffering believers are the flock of God set apart from the rest of the world. These are the orderly flock, redeemed to God by the Great Shepherd. They are also dignified with God's heritage, chosen out of the multitude of the people so that they can be His own people.

Believers are God's people. They should be treated with love, meekness, and tenderness, for the sake of Him. Jesus Christ hath bought them with his precious blood so that they can be partaker of His divine nature and forever live with Him in Heaven. Our Lord's Prayer is for all those who will believe in Him through the preaching of the Gospel that they may be one Him. "Father I want those you have given me to be with me where I am, and to see my glory, the glory you have given me because you loved me before the creation of the world" (John 17:24). The glory of Jesus Christ was His life of self-denying service and His dying on the Cross in order to redeem the entire human race. In the same way, the glory of all the believers is the path of humble service and bearing his or her cross with humility, self-denial and the willingness to suffer for Jesus Christ will ensure the true unity of believers and will lead to the true glory where they will forever live with Christ. Our Lord prays that God the Father to incorporate all the believers into one body as one in Christ because Christ is the head. Believers are His body no matter where every individual believer may be in nation of the Earth, and no matter whatever age they may be, either young or old, children, men or women, the God of all grace will unite believers in Christ as our head. He prayed that to God the Father while he was still on Earth to gather all the believers to Him as one and make believers one in Him What an immeasurable love of Jesus Christ that all the believers will be one with the Father, Son and the Holy Spirit forever.

    He prayed that all the believers should be bound together with love and charity and all to be of one heart. The oneness that is between Father and Son is to be manifested in all believers. Today it is taken for granted by some church the oneness of the Father and the Son, which was mentioned again and again. The Father loved the Son and the Son, always does what is pleasing to the Father, as the Father directed the Son, the action follows with the Spirit of obedience without measure. The Father and Son are one from the beginning of creation, designed in a unique way. The intimacy of this oneness is expressed in the words of Christ's prayer. As the pattern of that oneness, believers are one in some measure as God and Christ are one; they are united by a divine nature, by the power of divine grace in pursuance of the divine counsels of God. It is a holy union for holy ends; it is a complete union.

"The world and its desires pass away, but the man who does the will of God lives forever" (1st John 2:17). All things earthly things are fading and going to disappear one day; the things of the world are fading away and dying, but the immortality of the love of God will never fade away. The object of God's love compared to the opposition to the world passes away, abides forever. The love of God shall never fail; He himself is love. Whoever abides in Him lives in love, and the love of God will take us to Heaven to live with Him forever.

All those who believe in Jesus Christ should rejoice because He will never go back on his Word. Eternal life is waiting to those who call unto Him from the bottom of their heart sincerely and truthfully. All the Christians now and those who are going to be Christians until Christ's return will receive the blessing of eternal life. Hallelujah, come quickly Lord Jesus!

CHAPTER FIFTEEN

AWARENESS OF GOD IN OUR LIVES

God the Father Almighty, the compassionate and gracious God, all powerful, all knowing, all merciful and mighty, who is full of truth and righteousness, abounding in loving kindness, mercy and love. Our God has complete knowledge of everyone in the universe. All our thoughts and our actions are naked, open before Him. It is always good and rewarding to meditate on God's divine truths and God's will for our lives, applying it to ourselves in all the areas of our lives.

Believers should learn and practice how to lift their heart up in prayer to the Lord instead of occupying our mind with unprofitable, unfriendly, and unloving things. As we know that God is the all-knowing of all things. He is the Omniscient, which means that He is everywhere all the time. He is the Omnipresent; His truths must be acknowledged by all the people in the world. God who takes notice of every step we make, every right or wrong step we take. He is the ruler of all the souls of every human being on Earth. He knows which step and walk we walk either towards Him or far away from Him.

God knows when we moved away from Him and follow or keep bad company. He knows what is in every human heart. We either belong to Him or we belong to any ritual things of this world. There is not a word that we spoke that He does not know how the thought came to us and with what way we uttered it out.

Wherever we are, whatever we are doing, we are under the love and control of the eye and the hand of God. We cannot know how God searches or by what means He sees us. Wherever we may be, we are in His Garden, if we who believe in Him should think about this as well as those who says there is no God, they will stay away from evil and think no evil against each other.

People of this world should know that someone is watching over them every step of the way. As long as we are still in this tent, which means this body that our soul live in, we cannot see God, but God sees us perfectly every time. There is nothing, nothing we can hide us from the Almighty God. No clothe, no darkness, there is not any form of disguise that can hide us from God. He is the creator of Heaven and Earth and everything that He created obeys Him. He uses them as instruments to carry out His purposes.

The light cannot hide us. He see through the greatest light; He created the light. We believers must be very happy and rejoice because nothing can remove us from the sustaining hand of God and comforting presence of the Almighty God. Even if believers are persecuted and killed, his soul will ascend to Heaven and live with Christ forever.

Nothing can separate Him or her from the love of Jesus Christ the Savior who will raise the persecuted Christian's body to a glorious body. Nothing can separate believers from their Lord. Believers are always happy doing the service of the Lord by exercising strong faith, hope and with prayers. Jesus Christ is the Rock of salvation of those who believe in Him.

Hallelujah, because of Him and through Him, and to Him are all things that pertain to this world and knowledge, comfort, health, safety, progress, power and usefulness.

Let all His creation bless His Holy Name. Our first priority and goal on this Earth is to bless the Lord. The Earth is full of His praises and thankfulness. The sand at the sea shore, the flowers, the insects, animals, birds of the air, mountains, rivers, trees clouds, the sun, the moon, the stars, even to all the nine other planets from this Earth to Pluto, all must give his praises that due Him.

All the people of this Earth young and old, children, babies, household pets must give unceasing praises to God. All the servants of God, all the people of God must give him praises that is due Him. All places of His dominion must praise His Holy name. Everything on Earth and under the Earth must praise His Holy Name. Let all the ministers, pastors, reverends and ordain ministers preach and teach the true Gospel that will make the heart of people open and give themselves to the Almighty God.

Let them seek, knock, ask and pray to God in spirit and in truth forever and forever. The Spirit says: Come Lord Jesus.

SUMMARY

"Then I saw a new heaven and a new earth for the first heaven and the first earth had passed away, and there was no longer any sea, I saw the Holy City the New Jerusalem, coming down out of heaven from God, prepared as a bride beautifully dressed for her husband. And I heard a loud voice from the throne saying, now the dwelling of God is with men, and he will live with them. The will be his people, and God himself will be with them and be their God" (Revelation 21:1-3).

The final goal and the Scripture expectation of the redeemed is a new, transformed and redeemed world where Christ lives with His people and righteousness will reign in Holy perfection. In order to erase completely all the traces of sin and completely live eternally with the Lord in a new Earth and new Heaven, there will be a destruction of the Earth, stars and galaxies. Heaven and Earth will be shaken and will vanish like smoke; the stars will be dissolved and the elements destroyed as well. The new Earth will become the dwelling place of both humans and God. All the redeemed believers will possess bodies like Christ's which is a resurrection body, ones that are real, visible and tangible, but incorruptible and immortal. The New Jerusalem already exists in Heaven and it will soon come to Earth as the city of God for which Abraham and all God's faithful people have been waiting and of which God is the architect and the builder.

The new Earth will become God's dwelling place and He will remain with His people forever. The effect of sin such as sorrow, pain unhappiness and death will be gone forever; for the evils things of the first heaven and Earth will completely passed away. Believers, although remembering all things that are worth remembering, but they will not remember what caused them sorrow, because there will be no sorrow in the new Earth.

Eternal inheritance will be given to those who faithfully, and steadfastly, sincerely put their trust in Jesus Christ as the Savior of their soul. In order to make a way for the new Earth there will be a commencement of this new Earth while the old earth passed away. The blessed presence of God with his people will be proclaimed, the presence of God with His people in Heaven will not be interrupted as it is on Earth, but God will live with them continually. This new and blessed Earth will be free of all troubles and sorrow; all the causes of future sorrow shall be forever removed. God will wipe away every believer's tears.

All the multitudes of believers who are saved on Earth are saved in Heaven. God will have believers ranks and degrees of men in order to fill the heavenly mansions, high and low, those that are sanctified, the gate will be open on to them. In the New Jerusalem there will be a society that is perfectly pure. "There will be no more night. They will not need the light of a lamp or the light of the sun, for the Lord God will give them light. And they will reign for ever and ever" (Revelation 22:5). The believer's greatest blessing is that they will be pure in heart, for they will see God face to face as He is. All believers will have perfect knowledge of God and be joyful, walking in the light of the Lord; they will see clearly that Jesus Christ our Lord and Savior is the eternal life. Believe in Him and you will live for ever and ever. Amen, amen, amen.

GOD'S LOVING KINDNESS

God always give wealth, knowledge and wisdom to an individual with whom He wants them to share and He wants it to flow to others as a river or an ocean. He gave individuals great wisdom in so many areas of life such as wisdom and knowledge of engineering, technological innovations, medical breakthroughs with regards to so many diseases that plague people in the world. For example, the HIV medicine, the knowledge of teaching, hearing aids, eye transplants, kidney transplants and heart transplants, just to name a few.

He bestowed His favor upon Moses by answering Moses' prayer. He agreed to go with Moses and the people. All God's children should fervently pray, offer ceaseless prayers to know His ways, His heart, purpose, wisdom, holy knowledge, principles and even His suffering where we come to know God. God answered Moses' prayer because he respected him. He considered him as a friend, and he was pleased with him. Moses found favor because even though the people of Israel disobeyed God, Moses remained loyal and faithful to the Lord and mediated between the Lord and the people of Israel.

God changed King Saul's inner disposition through His anointing by the Holy Spirit. This change was unconditional or permanent, but something that could be maintained only by the Holy fellowship with a loving obedience to God. God's anointed King is Jesus, the Messiah, the Anointed One, whom God anointed with the Holy Spirit. All believers of Jesus Christ must be anointed with the same Holy Spirit as New Covenant priests and kings.

"While they were there, the time came for her to deliver her child. And she gave birth to her firstborn son and wrapped him in bands of cloth, and laid him in a manger, because there was no place for them in the inn. In that region there were shepherds living in the fields, keeping watch over their flock by night. Then an angel of the Lord stood before them and the glory of the Lord shone around them, and they were terrified. But the angel said to them, "Do not be afraid, for see I am bringing you good news of great joy for all the people. To you is born this day in the city of David a Savior, who is the Messiah, the Lord' " (Luke2:6-11). Christ the Lord has been anointed as the Messiah of God and the Lord who rules over His people.

Our actions toward those who are unkind to us such as the bully kids intentionally looking for some good kids to beat up in schools or in the neighborhood should be such that it might lead them to accept Christ as their Savior. Jesus Christ shows us this example when He was on the Cross. He prayed for His persecutors. Stephen, one of the first converted Christians when he was martyred, put Jesus' command into practice as he prayed for those who are stoning him before he died.

PRAYER OF INTERCESSOR FOR BELIEVERS

Lord Jesus Christ you are the eternal life. Bless all those who believe in you with a spirit of obedience, faithfulness and power of eternal life so that they can be able to live with you in Heaven above.

Open the heart and mind of all Christian leaders, pastors, and teachers of the Word of God to have a higher loyalty to you, so that they can live eternally with you in Heaven with the power of the indwelling of the Holy Spirit. Help all those who believe you to be complete in you O'Lord through the power of your eternal Spirit. You are the way, the truth and the life; all life dwells in you Lord Jesus Christ. Do not leave us, do not forsake us, let your full presence be revealed and be known in our lives.

Let the Holy Spirit empower all the believers and bring them closer and closer to you every day of their lives. Fulfill your great commission through all the believers so that the people of this Earth may know you and give their lives to you faithfully and sincerely.

Let them know that you are the Savior of all the living souls on Earth. Let the sinners be converted unto you every minute as the clock ticks; in so many ways, convert them right from the womb, all the infants, all children, young adults, adults and senior citizens.

I pray that you shine your great glory upon all believers and continue to fill them with your Spirit, with a spirit of holiness, faith, and joy throughout their days on Earth. In your matchless, great Holy Name, I pray. Amen.

BIOBLIOGRAPHY

Campbell, Morgan G,. The Parables of the Kingdom, New York, Fleming H. Revell Company (1907).

Dana, H. E. Searching the Scriptures. Kansas City Central Seminary press, (1946).

Evangelical Dictionary of Biblical Theology Evangelical Dictionary of Biblical Theology by Vlwell Baker Books Walter, 1973 Grand Rapids, Michigan (1973).

Fission, Floyd. Origin of the Gospel New York, Abingdon Press (1938).

Goodspeed, Edger J., An Introduction to New Testament, Chicago University of Chicago Press, (1937)

Hayes D. A., The Septic Gospel and Acts, New York: Methodist Book Concern, (1919). The Best Introduction to these four books of New Testament.

Hurter, A.M/, A. Pattern For Life. Philadelphia, Westminster Press, (1953).

Hynarale Donald P Husted, The Washing Church 190, Hope publishing.

MacDonald, William, Edited by Art Farstad, Believer's Bible Commentary Thomas Nelson Believer's Bible

Commentary William MacDonald Edited by Art Farstad Thomas Nelson Publishers

Matthew Henry Commentary in one Volume by Reo. Leslie For Church, Zondervan Publishing House (1960).

McDonald, William, Believers Bible Commentary, by William McDonald Edited by Aft Farstard – Thomas Nelson Publishers Nashville, Vancouver, London (1972).

Philip Yancey and Tim Stafford, The Student Bible Philip Yancey and Tim Stafford , New Revised Standard Version Published, Zondervan, 1994 Grand Rapids, Michigan USA (1994).

Ralph Earle, Exploring New Testament, Ralph Earle Beacon Hill Press (1955).

Smart ,James D, The Interpretation of Scripture, By James D. Smart

Student Study Bible NRSV Zondervan – Grand Rapids, Michigan USA (1994).

The Westminster Press Philadelphia USA October (2012).

BIBLICAL INDEX

PSALM 90:2, Psalm 10:16, Psalm 48:14, Psalm 119:89, Psalm 119:60, 16:11, 23:6

Deuteronomy 33:27

Isaiah 26:3-4, 5:17, 66:22, 53:6

Ezekiel 18:4

Jeremiah 10:10, 10:23

Genesis 6:1-22

Habakkuk 3:6

Luke 15:10

John 4:7-14, 3:1-9, 17:1-5, 17:3, 17:18, 11:25-26, 10:11

2nd Peter 2:17, 3:13,

1st Peter 5:10, 5:4

John 3:1-9, 17:1-5, 17:24

Romans 8:12-14, 6:1-4, 8:18, 6:23, 2:7

Hebrew 7:25-26, 7:16, 1:3, 9:12-15, 3:20-21

Ephesians 2:10, 4:20-24, 2:8-10, 1:14

Matthew 6:24

Mark 10:29-31

Galatians 5:22

2nd Corinthians 5:1, 4:17, 5:10

2nd Thessalonians 2:16

2nd Timothy 2:10, 4:8

1st John 2:25, 2:17

Revelation 21:1, 1-3, 22:5

Augustus M Toplady 1776

Books previously Published by the author
Grace Dola Balogun by
Grace Religious Books Publishing & Distributors, Inc.
New York

PRAYER THE SOURCE OF STRENGTH FOR LIFE - English Edition

Prayer the Source of Strength for Life is a powerful book that will energize your spirit to pray more and more until the prayer is part of your life and until the gate of heaven is opened and your prayer is answered. Your prayer life will change your life.

LA ORACION FUENTE DE FORTALEZA PARA LA VIDA – Spanish Edition.

Dios no's dio el poder de la oracion, quiere que lo usemos; debemos illamar, comunicarnos con el en todo lo que estemo spasando. El espera saber denosotros.

Spirit Power Volumes I and II

Spirit Power Volumes I and II both discuss the power of the Holy Spirit in the life of Believers.

The Power of the Spirit of God begins from the creation of the world up until today. That power will also continue until Christ returns to reign. Hallelujah

THE CROSS AND THE CRUCIFIXION

Our Lord Jesus Christ died on the Cross to bring forth love and compassion. Sin's impact on human life brings all other evil into our world, from one society to another society, from one culture to another.

But in Christ, we are clothed with His holiness. We have the gift of eternal life. The gate of heaven is open and we are eligible for our inheritance in heaven.

Hallelujah! Hosanna in the Highest. Jesus Christ paid it all, unto Him all we owe. The Cross of Christ is the Cross of joy, peace, and righteousness to all who believe in Him.

Three Simple Solutions for World Peace

Three Simple Solutions for World Peace is a book that clears all the confusion that many people of the world have been going through for many years. It is a book that gives light and advice to some of the problems that plague the world, and that offers solutions for these problems. It is a book that is full of knowledge, understanding and solutions that will bring some peace to the world.

Justification by Faith Alone in Christ Alone

Justification by Faith Alone in Christ Alone will clear all the confusion of believers' faith in Jesus Christ. Believers will also rejoice in the long sufferings – they will rejoice in their sufferings, afflictions, persecutions, rejections and all various trials that may press in on them because these long sufferings will help all the believers to be redeemed in Christ.

CHRISTIAN CELL PHONE SERIES:

Christian Cell Phone Godly Wisdom helps readers understand the role of God's wisdom and the importance of obtaining godly wisdom in one's life to produce prosperous results in all areas of life. These areas are critical and include family, relationships and finances. The acquiring of God's wisdom is to be sought after in life and will impact others as well.

Christian Cell Phone God's Favor is designed to give readers knowledge of God's favor from the Old Testament to the New Testament. With an analysis of the favor that was on Jesus, the Son of God, the reader will find that God's favor can completely change one's life and lead others to Christ as well.

Christian Cell Phone God's Anointing takes a look at the anointing on the life of Jesus that includes present day believers in Christ Jesus. This anointing can be applied to all areas of life and can be seen in miraculous ways. The anointing is what makes our life incredible and supernatural, drawing all those who see, to Christ.

JESUS CHRIST THE JOY OF CHRISTMAS

Jesus Christ the Joy of Christmas gives praise and tribute to the child that was born in Bethlehem. Tracing the prophecies of Old about this King that was born, the author gives an account of the sinless Lamb of God who came to take away the peoples' sin from a biblical perspective, who is the real Joy of Christmas.

PRAYER FOR THE BULLY VICTIMS AND THE BULLY TOO!

Prayer for the Bully Victims and the Bully Too addresses the issue of the bully from the classroom to the home. By the use of scriptural application, the author takes a look at what can be done to help the bully kid and their victims. The author has written several key prayers that readers can use to help either the bully victim or parents' who are dealing with a child that has become a bully.

I AM THE RESURRECTION AND THE LIFE

Powerful, inspirational and written from a firm biblical perspective, multi-published author Grace Dola Balogun, gives life to others through the power of Jesus Christ who is the Resurrection and the life. This book will open eyes to the amazing and abundant blessings of accepting Jesus Christ as your Lord and Savior, giving keen insight into the Scriptures on the power available to all through the Holy Spirit with an emphasis on aspects of eternal life for the believer.

About the Author

Grace Dola Balogun graduated from Fordham University Graduate School of Religion and Religious Education in the year 2010 with an M.A. in Religion and Religious Education. She has been a prayer mentor and advisor for many Christians of all denominations for many years.

Visit her online at:
www.Gracereligiousbookspublishers.com
Facebook
Twitter @prayersource

To order additional copies of this book, please E-mail: info@gracereligiousbookspublishers.com.

This book may also be ordered from 30,000 wholesalers, retailers, and booksellers in the U. S., and in Canada and over 100 countries globally.

To contact Grace Dola Balogun for an interview or a speaking engagement, please E-mail:

info@gracereligiousbookspublishers.com

I AM THE ETERNAL LIFE

The Spirit and the bride say,
"Come!" And let the one who hears say, "Come!" Let the
one who is thirsty come;
and let the one who wishes take the free
gift of the water of life (Revelation 22:17).

MARANATHA EVEN SO COME LORD JESUS (1ST CORINTHIANS 16:22, REVELATION 22:20)

I AM THE ETERNAL LIFE

ORDER FORM

TO ORDER YOUR COPY OF ANY BOOK:

NAME:_____

ADDRESS:_____

_____

TELEPHONE:_____

FAX#:_____

MAIL:_____

QUANTITY:_____

MAIL TO:

Grace Religious Books Publishing & Distributors, Inc.
New York
213 Bennett Avenue
New York, NY 10040

I AM THE ETERNAL LIFE

www.ingramcontent.com/pod-product-compliance
Lightning Source LLC
Chambersburg PA
CBHW052053070526
44584CB00017B/2151